Invitation and Encounter

INVITATION AND ENCOUNTER

EVANGELIZING THROUGH THE SACRAMENTS

Timothy P. O'Malley

Our Sunday Visitor
Huntington, Indiana

Nihil Obstat
Msgr. Michael Heintz, Ph.D.
Censor Librorum

I*mprimatur*
✠ Kevin C. Rhoades
Bishop of Fort Wayne-South Bend
January 20, 2022

The *Nihil Obstat* and *Imprimatur* are official declarations that a book is free from doctrinal or moral error. It is not implied that those who have granted the *Nihil Obstat* and *Imprimatur* agree with the contents, opinions, or statements expressed.

Our Sunday Visitor Publishing Division
Our Sunday Visitor, Inc.
200 Noll Plaza
Huntington, IN 46750
1-800-348-2440
ISBN: 978-1-68192-777-0 (Inventory No. T2647)
1. RELIGION—Christian Rituals & Practice—Sacraments.
2. RELIGION—Christianity—Catholic.
3. RELIGION—Christian Ministry—Evangelism.

eISBN: 978-1-68192-778-7
LCCN: 2022933570

Cover design: Tyler Ottinger
Cover art: Adodestock
Interior design: Amanda Falk

PRINTED IN THE UNITED STATES OF AMERICA

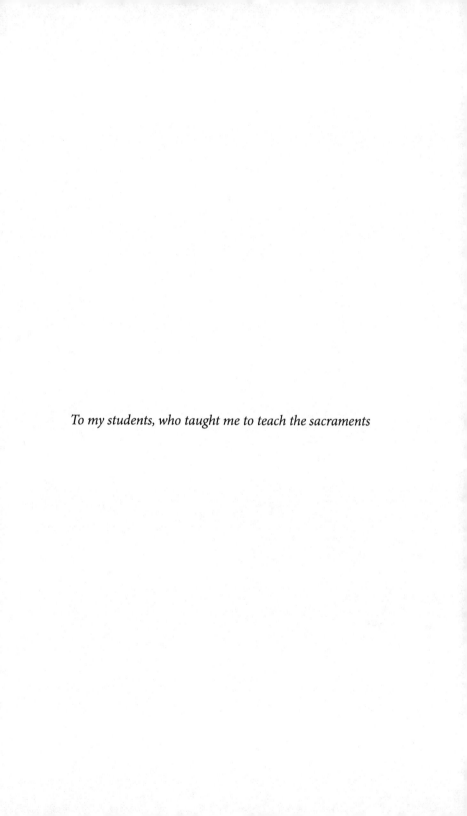

To my students, who taught me to teach the sacraments

Contents

CHAPTER 1
Sacramentalized and Evangelized   13

Introduces readers to the Catechism of the Catholic Church's definition of a sacrament as a sacred sign — instituted by Christ and entrusted to the Church — whereby divine life is dispensed, showing how this definition is linked to the Church's mission of evangelization.

CHAPTER 2
Our Identity as Priests of Christ:
Baptism, Confirmation, and Holy Orders   31

Focuses on the three sacraments that bestow a character or a permanent mark: baptism, confirmation, and holy orders. Proposes that these sacraments change our identity, capacitating each of the faithful to participate in Christ's priesthood.

CHAPTER 3
The Eucharist and the Sacrifice of Time   57

Explores how the Eucharist is a common act of the entire Church, enabling every member of Christ's Body to understand anew the relationship between past, present, and future. Shows how this sacrament is integral to the priestly identity of the People of God.

CHAPTER 4
Marriage as the Transformation
of the Mundane

Traces the history of marriage in the Church. Proposes that marriage points toward the meaning of the entire sacramental system of the Church, the transformation of all creation into a space where divine love may dwell.

CHAPTER 5
Sin and Death: Consecrating
Our Diminishments

Considers how the rite of penance and the anointing of the sick allow us to heal from the suffering of sin and death. Shows how the reception of these sacraments proposes to the entire Church the power of God to redeem every aspect of human life.

CHAPTER 6
Cultivating Dispositions
for a Sacramental Life

Concludes by returning to the original thesis: Sacraments consecrate us to offer our lives as a spiritual sacrifice. Suggests ways of engaging in sacramental formation to dispose men and women to the evangelizing power of the sacraments.

Introduction

The sacraments of the Catholic Church capture the imagination. Think about how the Church is often depicted in movies. When you want to evoke Catholicism to a moviegoer, the camera focuses upon incense during a Mass or a penitent waiting outside a confessional. If you were to approach a random person on the street, asking him or her to describe five characteristics of the Catholic Church, your random interviewee would likely mention one of the sacraments.

And yet, what is a sacrament, and why do the sacraments matter so much to Catholics? For us today, this question is not merely theoretical. In the past several years, Catholic participation in the sacraments has seen significant decline in the United States. Between 2015 and 2019, there were 110,000 fewer infant baptisms, 7,000 fewer adult baptisms, 10,000 fewer confirmations, 126,000 fewer first Communions, and 11,000 fewer marriages.[1] With COVID-19, these numbers are likely now even lower. You do not need to be a sociologist to recognize that the Church in the United States is experiencing a crisis related to the sacraments.

The decline in sacramental life in the United States has often been explained through a popular phrase in pastoral circles. The Church is full of those who have been "sacramentalized but not evangelized." That is, they have received the sacraments as children without experiencing a personal relationship with Jesus Christ. The sacraments function for such persons as cultural rites of passage, and when one is no longer connected to Catholic culture, then those rites of passage become meaningless and therefore unnecessary. The data support this assumption, since the most significant declines are seen in the sacraments that have traditionally been associated with rites of passage: infant baptism and first Communion. Many parents, who in the past would have carried on the faith of their own childhoods and initiated their children in the sacraments, are not doing so. Such parents are sacramentalized but not evangelized.

Still, there is a theological problem with the phrase "sacramentalized but not evangelized." It is true that the sacraments are not magical, initiating someone into faith against his or her will. But this has never been the understanding of the sacraments, at least not among theologians. The Church teaches that sacraments effect salvation, but they do so because Jesus Christ is the source of the sacramental life.

Sometimes people in the pews and even clergy forget this. The sacraments can become nothing more than rites of passage, things we do because our families expect us to. The Church has sought to respond to this assumption throughout history, but especially over the last hundred years. Beginning in the early twentieth century, a personalist account of the sacraments was offered by the Church, one in which sacramental celebrations are understood as encounters with Jesus Christ. In this approach, the Church emphasizes that my person is transformed through liturgical and sacramental worship. The sacraments, therefore, are always evangelizing, because they make available the salvation offered by Jesus Christ to the Church and to the world. The sacraments change the identity of the person, conforming him or her completely to Christ. Pope Saint Pius X, one of the great figures who contributed to sacramental renewal in the Church, had as his motto "to restore all things in Christ."

This book will therefore consider the sacraments of the Church as moments of evangelization — occasions in which our humanity is redeemed through an encounter with Jesus Christ, in which he acts through our very bodies. Sacraments are always encounters with Jesus through the signs and symbols of the liturgy — and they effect salvation. In the recently updated *Directory for Catechesis*, the document states:

> Evangelization has as its ultimate aim the fulfillment of human life. In presenting this teaching, the Christian West has used the category of salvation, while the Christian East has preferred to speak of *divinization*. Why did God become human? "To save us," says the West. "So that the human being may become God," affirms the East. These two expressions, in reality, are complementary: God became human, so that humanity could become truly human as he intended and created him to be; humanity, whose icon is the Son; the human being, who is saved from evil and death, in order to participate in the divine nature. Believers can already experience this salvation here and now, but it will find its fullness in the resurrection.[2]

If we are to cultivate renewed commitment to the sacramental life, it will be because we present the sacraments of Catholicism not as isolated rites of passage, but as material ways in which the Triune God invites men and women to experience salvation here and now. The sacraments are the way that human beings are invited to become divine.

In this book, we will be guided by figures from throughout the twentieth century who taught us to see the sacraments of the Church as personal encounters with divine love. Sacramental theology, after all, is not just an extension of canon law — that is, the official rule book of the Church. Rather, sacramental theology (even when using technical language) invites every member of the Church to experience a new evangelization made possible by the sacraments.

Chapter 1

Sacramentalized
and Evangelized

An introduction to the sacraments, emphasizing the potential for sacramental evangelization, will require special attention given to each of the seven sacraments of the Catholic Church. But before we turn to each of the individual sacraments, we must grasp the definition of a sacrament. According to the *Catechism of the Catholic Church:*

> The sacraments are efficacious signs of grace, instituted by Christ and entrusted to the Church, by which divine life is dispensed to us. The visible rites by which the sacraments are celebrated signify and make present the graces proper to each sacrament. They bear fruit in those who receive them with the required dispositions.[1]

This definition is rich, worthy of closer attention. What do we mean when we say that sacraments are efficacious signs of grace? How are they instituted by Christ? What authority does the Church have over the sacraments? What is the divine life that is dispensed to us? What is the relationship between the sacraments, grace, and the liturgical rites? What does sacramental fruitfulness look like? And what does all of this have to do with evangelization?

Efficacious Signs

The language of signification is essential to the sacraments of the Church. Sacraments are signs. But what is a sign? Imagine that I want to direct your attention to the setting sun. We are outside, and it is too noisy for you to hear me. So, I tap you on the shoulder and point to the sun. You recognize what I have done, and you turn your attention to the beautiful sunset. My act of communication to you consists of signs. Tapping you on the shoulder has a meaning beyond the physicality of the encounter. You recognize the "significance" of the shoulder tap and of my pointed finger, realizing that I am saying to you, "Look at that!"

Sacraments are signs in a similar way. Except, they are acts of communication, not from a human teacher, but from God. Think about the water that is used in baptism. In our experience, what is water? It is not just a material substance that we consume when we are dehydrated. Rather, it has a meaning that is not reducible to its physicality. If you are traveling through a desert, and are dying from thirst, water is a sign of life. If your home is flooded during a horrendous rainstorm, you recognize the destructive power of water. If you are experiencing a dreadful drought in the summer months, a drop of rain is the manifestation of hope. These meanings are not simply constructed by human beings, who want to see more in water than is there. Rather, Catholics profess that the God who created all things out of love has given us a world full of meaning.

This account of signification describes what the Church has called "creation sacraments." Creation sacraments reveal to us that there is no other way that God reveals himself to us as embodied creatures than through materiality. As Joseph Ratzinger — later Pope Benedict XVI — wrote in an article on the sacraments, "The sacrament in its universal form in the history of religion is therefore at first simply the expression of the experience that God encounters man in a human way."[2] The sacraments are "signs" because the whole created order is taken up to communicate God's love to men and women.

Often, we hear theologians describe "sacramentality" as nothing more than the presence of God in the created world. But this is an insufficient account of sacramentality. After all, the sacraments are not merely signs indicating that God is cosmically present in mountain peaks, sun-kissed valleys, or the shining sea. The sacraments are, moreover, signs that point concretely to God's intimate involvement in the history of Israel and the Church.

Think again about the waters of baptism. The blessing prayer over the baptismal waters recalls the primordial waters of creation in Genesis, Israel's passing dry-shod through the Red Sea, the water that flowed from the rock in the Book of Exodus, and the baptism of Jesus Christ in the Jordan River. The sacraments are not just signs of God as creator of the universe; rather, the sacraments are signs that point toward what God has done in history. Again, turning to Joseph Ratzinger: "For the Christian sacraments mean not only insertion into the God-permeated cosmos ... they mean at the same time insertion into the history that originates in Christ."[3] The waters of baptism are meaningful because they are signs of life and death that have been taken up by Jesus Christ in his life, death, and resurrection. And through our encounter with the signs in the sacraments, we are "inserted" into the history of God's saving love.

How so? To answer this question, we need to understand the second dimension of the sacraments. They are not only "signs" but *efficacious* signs of grace. The sacraments signify (that is, they communicate the divine presence), but they also "do something" (that is, they integrate us into God's love).

How can we be integrated into a history that is in the past? In some ways, this is a driving question addressed by every school curriculum. How does one learn to see oneself as a citizen of the United States or Mexico? One must both learn the history of that country and to appropriate it. I fully become a citizen of the United States when I not only remember the history of the American Revolution, but recognize it as "my history."

This analogy of the sacraments works to an extent. Much like learning what it means to be a U.S. citizen, I do participate in the past of Christ's life, death, and resurrection when I see it as integral to my own identity, here and now. I have appropriated this story into my life, making it my own.

But when the Church calls the sacraments "efficacious signs of grace," the Church means something more than a subjective appropriation of the history of salvation. During baptism, it is not only a person who grasps the fullness of baptism in the history of salvation who receives grace, but, rather, *anyone* who asks to be baptized in the name of the Father, the Son, and the Holy Spirit receives the grace of the sacrament. Something objective happens through the sacraments, and this occurs regardless of how much or how little the individual person understands about the power of that sacrament. A sinner is forgiven (penance), bread and wine become Christ's Body and Blood (the Eucharist), and a man and a woman are united in a sacramental union (matrimony). God gives grace through the sacraments, whether we are ready to receive it or not.

The sacraments are objectively efficacious because of the

uniqueness of Jesus Christ. Likely, you have heard the term *hypostatic union*. The hypostatic union refers to the mystery of the Incarnation, the Word becoming flesh and dwelling among us. The *Catechism* says about the Incarnation and the hypostatic union that "Jesus Christ possesses two natures, one divine and the other human, not confused, but united in the one person of God's Son."[4] Jesus Christ is fully human and fully divine, without those two natures mixing with one another. No other person who has ever existed can make this claim.

Because of the hypostatic union (the joining together of two natures — or *hypostases* — in the single person of God's Son), Christ's humanity becomes an instrument for communicating divine life, or grace. A nineteenth-century theologian, Matthias Scheeben (someone we will encounter a lot in this book), describes why this is important for us:

> The humanity of Christ is able to operate in a supernatural manner within itself, and also to perform acts which are of supernatural benefit to all creatures and to achieve much that in itself can be effected only by the infinite power of God. Thus the humanity of Christ can communicate to others the supernatural life which it possesses itself. ... In brief, the hypostatic union enables the humanity of Christ to acquire for others ... and to produce in them its own supernatural prerogatives.[5]

What does Scheeben mean? Jesus Christ's human actions are also divine actions. When Christ sheds tears at the tomb of Lazarus, it is the God-man who is crying. Due to the Incarnation of Christ, the natural sorrow we experience in human life has been assumed by God. Tears have been consecrated or sanctified. All that is human, except for sin, has been assumed by Jesus Christ. He was born as a babe in a manger in Bethlehem, knew the sorrow of the death of his father Joseph, feasted with his disciples, experienced love for his mother, and trembled with fear in the Garden of Gethsemane. Through Christ, everything that is human may become divine. The natural dimensions of human life may be elevated beyond what any human being can imagine possible. They may become "supernatural." Supernatural does not refer to the kind of books that one might find in a New Age section of a bookstore. Rather, the supernatural is that which transcends anything creaturely. It is beyond what any creature could do on his or her own; the transcendent is God's own activity. Because Jesus Christ is the God-man who consecrates all that is human to the Father, he is the perfect mediator between God and humanity. He transforms the natural (the simply human) into the supernatural (that which transcends humanity) through his whole life. This is what the Church means when she speaks about the Paschal Mystery.[6] Through Jesus Christ's life, death, and resurrection, men and women pass over into the grace, or gift, of divine life. Jesus' sacrifice of himself upon the cross, his resurrection, and his Ascension into heaven does something for all of us. Jesus Christ makes it possible for us as mere mortals to worship God perfectly — to make our embodied, material, all so human history into a living sacrifice to God. As Scheeben writes:

> In accordance with God's plan, the entire life and existence of Christ were essentially devoted to His sublime sacrificial worship. By taking possession of His human nature He made His own the object He was to offer, and by uniting it to His person He invested it with an infinite value. By His Passion and death, which He had in mind during His whole earthly career, He accomplished its immolation. By His resurrection and glorification, He made it a holocaust. Finally, by His ascension He transferred it to heaven, and placed it at the feet of His Fa-

ther, that it might be His as the eternal pledge of perfect
worship.[7]

In his Paschal Mystery, Jesus Christ functions as the perfect
priest. His humanity is not left behind at the Ascension, discard-
ed as something that he no longer needs. The perfect represen-
tative of humanity, Jesus Christ, continues to offer the sacrifice
of love to the Father.

For this reason, the events of the Paschal Mystery are never
solely in the past. Remember our question: How can we experience a past event in the present? Ascended into heaven, Jesus
Christ is the great High Priest who even now offers a perfect
sacrifice of his Flesh and Blood to the Father. As we read in the
Second Vatican Council's constitution on the Church, *Lumen
Gentium*:

> In the human nature united to Himself the Son of God,
> by overcoming death through His own death and resur-
> rection, redeemed man and re-molded him into a new
> creation. By communicating His Spirit, Christ made His
> brothers, called together from all nations, mystically the
> components of His own Body. ... In that Body the life of
> Christ is poured into the believers who, through the sac-
> raments, are united in a hidden and real way to Christ
> who suffered and was glorified.[8]

The Church, celebrating the sacraments, is not reducible to a human society performing sacred rites. Rather, the Church is the
mystical Body of Christ. She is united to Jesus as the Bridegroom
through the gift of the Spirit. What the Church does, Christ also
does. That means that when one is baptized in the Church, it
is Jesus Christ who is doing the baptism through the words of
the minister and the sign of water. Having been baptized, the

Christian now belongs to the Church, which is Christ's Body. There is an objective change that takes place in the identity of the baptized. And the vocation of those who are baptized is now to make their lives into a living sacrifice of praise to the Father.

This efficacious change is not to be separated from the signification of the sacraments. The sacraments effect by signifying. Water cleanses. It destroys. It quenches one's thirst. Christ uses the very material significance of water to bestow the gift of new life. Baptism cleanses one from sin. It destroys all that keeps one away from God. It quenches the thirst of one who longs for perfect union with God. The gift, or grace, of baptism is inseparable from these material significations. At the same time, Jesus himself was baptized in the Jordan. He was announced as the beloved son of the Father at his baptism. So too baptism makes us into beloved sons and daughters of God, sharing Christ's life with the Father.

Therefore, sacraments are efficacious signs. They bestow the gift of divine union to men and women. They make that which is natural, supernatural. They are efficacious, because it is always the God-man, Jesus Christ, through the power of the Spirit, who acts in the sacraments. And God does all of this through the material signs of the sacraments.

Instituted by Christ and Entrusted to the Church

Catholics teach that there are seven sacraments that have been instituted by Christ. The language of "instituted by" does not mean that Jesus passed out liturgical books for each of the sacraments to the twelve apostles. Rather, Jesus Christ instituted, or established, the sacraments as described in the previous section. His entire life was like a sacrament, in which his humanity was an efficacious sign of grace. When Jesus fed the hungry masses with heavenly bread, when he healed the sick, when he called the twelve apostles, when he attended the wedding at Cana, when he breathed his Spirit over creation upon the cross, Jesus was instituting the sacraments. The Church, as the Body of Christ, still makes the sacramental presence of Jesus available to the world today.

And yet, the Church does speak of seven *precise* sacraments. This recognition of seven sacraments was not immediate in the history of the Church. What were referred to as "sacraments" in the early Church often referred to any sacred sign. In early medieval Catholicism, the consecration of a king was considered to be one of the seven sacraments. At an English coronation, consecrated oil is still poured upon the head of the reigning monarch. And yet, the Church today does not recognize coronation as one of the sacraments. In early medieval thought, marriage was not yet universally recognized as a sacrament, but often understood simply as a state akin to the consecrated life. Marriage was discerned as one of the sacraments through the development of medieval canon law and theology.

The gradual development of the sacramental system has led some theologians to think about this development as an accident of history. According to this line of thought, there are seven sacraments only because the Church has said so. That means that there could be two sacraments, twelve sacraments, or one hundred and twenty sacraments.

St. Thomas Aquinas takes up this question in his work, the *Summa Theologiae*. In Question 65 of the third part of the *Summa*, Saint Thomas asks why there should be seven sacraments. Assuming that the Church is right to teach that there are seven sacraments, Saint Thomas seeks to understand why this teaching is fitting, apt, or reasonable. Importantly, Saint Thomas argues that it is apt because the sacraments are intended to sanctify the entirety of human life, from birth to death. Because human beings are embodied creatures, this spiritual renewal of the person must find its analogue in bodily life. He writes, "For spiritual life has a certain conformity with the life of the body; just as other corporeal things have a certain likeness to things spiritual."[9] Since human life begins with birth, or generation, then the spiritual life also must commence with generation. Hence, the first Sacrament of Baptism. After birth, we begin to grow and mature. This spiritual maturation is bestowed in the Sacrament of Confirmation. We only continue growing, of course, through nourishment, and therefore, the Eucharist is the sacrament that spiritually nourishes us.

We know all too well that human life is not reducible to infinite growth and progress. We experience sickness. The Sacraments of both Penance and Extreme Unction (a rite that we more often call Anointing of the Sick) are intended as occasions for healing us of spiritual illness. We sin, thus harming our spiritual lives. Our impending mortality requires us to recognize our own fragility, requiring grace to prepare ourselves to meet God face-to-face.

Lastly, the sacraments are not only directed toward the spiritual life of the individual. Rather, the sacraments are intended to sanctify the common life of the Church. The Sacrament of Holy Orders bestows the authority upon priests to offer the sacrifice of the Eucharist and all the sacraments for the sake of the Body of Christ. For Saint Thomas, this includes the authority of both teaching and governing. There is also the Sacrament of Marriage, which is related to the natural propagation of the species. Through marriage, the Church receives new life, both through the generation of children who are baptized, and through the spiritual fruitfulness of the nuptial union.

It is ultimately fitting that there are seven sacraments, because the sacraments should heal and sanctify the entirety of human life from birth to death. The seven sacraments represent, like the seven days of creation, the perfection of the created order. There are seven sacraments (or sacred signs) instituted by

Christ, which effect grace through signifying, because human beings must spiritually grow in an analogous way to how we grow physically. Importantly, the sacraments, for Saint Thomas, are not the only way that human beings are sanctified in this life. Sacramentals, such as the consecration of an altar, the use of holy water, and even religious consecration dispose us to participate more fully in the sacramental life. They are holy things, without themselves being one of the seven sacraments, that unite us to the presence of Christ in the Scriptures.

The sacraments, instituted by Christ, are also entrusted to the Church. The Church has "authority" over the administration of the sacraments, including the liturgical rites. This authority, of course, is not reducible to raw power. The sole authority of the Church comes from Jesus Christ. The Church regulates the sacraments not through a will to power, but by means of reflecting on the sacraments exclusively in light of the Word of God, that is, Scripture and Tradition. Jesus Christ tells us in the Gospel of Matthew that we are to baptize in the name of the Father, the Son, and the Holy Spirit. Baptism in Scripture and Tradition includes water. The Church cannot decide that baptism would be better with Jell-O or white wine. The Church cannot baptize in the name of a community rather than the Father, the Son, and the Holy Spirit.

The reformed rites of the Second Vatican Council, through a process of studying Scripture and Tradition, did make liturgical changes around each of the sacraments. The Nuptial Blessing in the marriage rite before the Second Vatican Council did not include an explicit blessing of the husband. Through reflection upon Scripture and Tradition, the Church developed a blessing that is now given to both the husband and the wife. But the rites did not change the form of the sacrament, which is the exchange of consent between husband and wife. Within the next two hundred years, the liturgical rites of marriage may change again through liturgical development. But the Roman Catholic Church cannot, without contradicting what constitutes the Sacrament of Marriage, decide that nuptial consent is optional to the sacrament as it has developed in the West.

For this reason, it is wise for the Church to remember that the sacraments are entrusted to the Church, because the sacraments are at the heart of what the Church is. The Church is not exclusively a human society, but the mystical Body of Christ. We receive our identity, as members of this Church, as a gift from God. Therefore, the rituals of the sacraments should be treated as gifts, rather than creative opportunities to express our personal faith. A bishop, priest, or deacon should not change the words of the Eucharistic Prayer or the Nuptial Blessing because he wants to. He is not giving himself in the sacraments; rather, he is giving Jesus Christ as mediated through the Church.

Grace, Divine Life, and the Sacramental Rites

In sacramental catechesis, one frequently hears an analogy for the sacraments that is a bit problematic. The sacraments, in this analogy, are like sports drinks (such as Gatorade or Powerade). Just as drinking Gatorade gives us a boost of energy while playing football, the sacraments give us a boost while living the Christian life.

The problem with this approach is that it treats sacramental grace as a quantity rather than an invitation to a personal encounter with God. According to this way of thinking, when we eat Christ's Body and Blood, we receive "this bit" of grace that will sustain us throughout the week. The more sacraments we receive, the "more grace" we get.

And yet, God does not "bestow grace" in a quantifiable way. Rather, we should understand the word "grace" as linked to its Latin origin in the word *gratia*, which means "by the grace of God." Grace is a gift bestowed upon us by God. And as we know analogically from human gift-giving, when we give a gift, we are giving part of ourselves. If I buy a ring for my spouse, I am ideally not just giving her some random object that is worth a certain amount of money. I am proclaiming that in this gift, I give myself to you. The ring is a self-gift, a pledge of love.

With God, the link between the gift and the giver is even closer, because of who God is. The gift that is given in each sacrament is a relationship with God, who is Father, Son, and Holy Spirit. Grace is the gift of sharing or participating in divine life. As Matthias Scheeben writes, "By the reception of a sacrament the recipient enters into a special relationship with the God-man as his head, and by virtue of this relationship must also, as a member, share in the power of his head."[10] So, in baptism, we receive the "grace" or "gift" of the forgiveness of sin. This gift is bestowed so that men and women can enter into union with Jesus Christ through the power of the Holy Spirit. Grace is offered for each of us so that we may become a son or daughter of God, a gift that no human being could perform by him- or herself. Such holiness, this transformation of identity, must be given by the giver of all gifts, the triune God.

The sacraments, therefore, are mysteries of Christ and the Church. The Latin word *sacramentum* is a translation of the Greek word *musterion*, or mystery. Christian mystery, according to Matthias Scheeben, "must of necessity lie absolutely beyond the reach of reason. ... These suprarational truths are more sublime, more precious, more valuable than purely rational truths."[11] The mysteries of Christianity cannot be known through human reason, because they relate to God's surprising, remarkable, and unfathomable decision to enter into relationship with us. Relationships, generally, transcend the boundaries of human reason. The love of my spouse cannot be measured as one measures the quantity of acid or base in a chemical experiment. I cannot use formal logic to determine if my wife loves me. And even more so, one cannot determine from human reason that God would take flesh, die upon the cross, unite himself to the Church, and make available to us his Body and Blood through the Eucharist. All of this is a surprising, remarkable, and unfathomable gift of grace. It is a mystery.

The sacraments are mysteries of divine love; therefore, sacramental theology must avoid a rational reductionism that treats the sacraments as mechanical acts alone. It's not as if we take this bit of water, say these words, and we have a Christian. The sacraments, because they are mysteries of grace, are always personal encounters with the God who gives himself to us in love. That is why the sacraments are evangelizing. They are God's gift of love to us, here and now.

And for this reason, the liturgical rites by which the sacraments are celebrated are part of this excessive, divine gift of love. Yes, the heart of the Eucharist is the eating and drinking of Christ's Body and Blood, a union with God that sustains us as we pursue perfect love. The other actions of the Mass dispose us to fully receive this gift of love. Beautiful churches, well-prayed prayers, incense rising to heaven, music that is appropriately sacred, a consecrated altar, the statues of angels and saints, and a tabernacle lamp are all ordered to the reception of the sacramental grace of the Eucharist.

Sacramental Fruitfulness

In every sacrament, the gift of divine love is given to us through the working of Jesus Christ. And yet, just as a spouse may respond to a gift from a husband or wife with ingratitude, we may reject the gift offered by God in the sacrament. This is what the Church means when she speaks about sacramental fruitfulness. The gift is always given by God, but the one receiving the gift may not benefit from the offer of love.

Once again, let us think about the Sacrament of Baptism. An

infant may receive from the Church the gift of salvation offered by Christ. That infant has his or her identity changed, becoming a member of Christ's Body. But that infant may grow up in such a way that he or she has no further contact with the Church. The gift of love, the grace of union with Christ, has been given. God gives, because God is infinitely generous. The grown child would need to have the proper dispositions to experience baptism as sacramentally fruitful. The baptized Christian is consecrated to God, ordered toward divine worship. For that sacrament to be fruitful, the child who has received the Sacrament of Baptism would need to develop dispositions of faith, hope, and love. He or she would need to want to worship God, to recognize that every dimension of human life is a gift from God. The child would need to see the Church herself as a gift, and membership in that Body as integral to his or her identity. When babies are baptized, parents and godparents pledge themselves to cultivating these dispositions.

Yet, even though the fruitfulness of the sacrament depends on these dispositions, there is still the objective value of the sacrament when it is bestowed. Even if the parents do not nurture the faith of their child, or even if the ordained minister who performs the baptism is secretly a terrible person, the child nonetheless has been baptized. To use the technical language that the Church employs in sacramental theology, the sacrament "happens" simply through doing what the Church intends in that sacrament. The Latin term for this is *ex opere operato* — literally "from the work being worked." Because Jesus Christ is the God-man who sanctifies all humanity, the offer of love is given. It is Christ at work in the sacraments, not the ordained minister alone. There is a power to the sacrament that is not dependent on us; this power is what sacramental theology calls the *opus operatum* — literally "the work worked." And yet, sacramental theology also recognizes that human beings must allow themselves to participate in God's work. We must not only praise God in a mechanical way, but we must long to praise God. The Church calls our task in the sacraments the *opus operantis* — the disposition that we cultivate to receive God's gracious gift.

For example, in marriage, in speaking the words of consent, in giving ourselves to our spouses, the love of Christ and the Church binds the couple together. This is the *opus operatum*. The work is done, it is given through the power of Christ and the Spirit. But the couple cannot expect to bear fruit from this bond if they never pray together, or if they cheat on one another, or harbor hatred toward one another. One must understand what this bond of love is, participate regularly in the Eucharistic sacrifice, celebrate penance, and share every dimension of life together as a sacrifice of love. This cultivation of a fruitful spiritual life is the *opus operantis*.

By extension, for Christians who are sacramentally united to Jesus Christ, there is no work that we do exclusively on our own. Even our desire to go to Mass is not our own work. Rather, it is already a gift from the Holy Spirit, which disposes us to receive the totality of divine love in the Blessed Sacrament.

So, there is a way in which it is acceptable to think about being sacramentalized, but not evangelized. Yet, it is better to say that we have received the sacraments, but the sacraments have not yet born fruit from a life of faith, hope, and love. Catechesis may invite us to better understand what happened to us in the sacraments, and how we may begin to bear fruit through the pursuit of holiness. Then, the latent (or hidden) evangelizing power of the sacraments will become patent (or visible).

As we have seen, the sacraments are, by their nature, evangelizing. They are sacred signs that allow us to enter into a relationship with Christ, transforming our very identity. The sacraments allow our flesh and blood lives to become fruitful, a fragrant offering of love for the life of the world. For this reason, to celebrate the sacraments is a supreme act of evangelization. In the following chapters, we will explore how each of the sacraments function in this evangelizing way as efficacious signs that bestow grace, usher us into divine life, and bear fruit for those who receive them with the required dispositions.

Chapter 2
Our Identity as Priests of Christ: Baptism, Confirmation, and Holy Orders

Parents often agonize over the names that they will bestow upon their children. After all, naming is a big deal. The child likely will be called that name for the rest of his or her life. Being called "Tim" (or when I was younger, "Timmy") is not just the way that people get my attention in a crowd, but is integral to my identity.

If we are to address the role of evangelization in the sacraments, we must first begin with the theme of identity. The sacraments, as we saw in the previous chapter, are not only rites of passage. They are occasions in which Jesus Christ works through the Church by means of efficacious signs for the salvation of men and women.

The sacraments in this second chapter relate to how a person's identity is transformed through baptism, confirmation, and holy orders. In the Sacrament of Baptism, the Christian is baptized in the name of the Father, the Son, and the Holy Spirit. The baptized child or adult has his or her identity fundamentally changed through the sacrament. The baptized person is now a priest, a prophet, and a royal figure who is to consecrate all the world to God. Baptism initiates one into what the Church calls the "spiritual priesthood of the faithful." Confirmation is a strengthening of this priestly identity, a maturation that comes through a further outpouring of the Holy Spirit. Holy orders is linked closely to both baptism and confirmation, because a new identity is given to an ordained man for the benefit of the Church so that he may bestow upon the priestly people the divine love available through all the sacraments.

Thus, these three sacraments are linked to the identity of the whole Church as a priesthood of the faithful. Baptism and confirmation are not mere rites of passage, such as how we celebrate the birth of a new child or recognize the maturation of adolescence. They are sacraments that order the human being — at whatever age they are received — "to present your bodies as a living sacrifice, holy and acceptable to God, which is your spiritual worship" (Rom 12:1). Baptism and confirmation are intrinsically related to evangelization because they consecrate the person as a member of a spiritual priesthood. Holy orders is a ministerial function, given by Christ through the Church, to the man who now acts in the name of Christ and the Church (*in persona Christi et ecclesiae*). He no longer acts exclusively in his own name, out of his own identity, but out of an identity given by Christ through the Sacrament of Holy Orders. This identity is not earned, but bestowed as gift for the sake of the entire faithful. Holy orders, for this reason too, is a supremely evangelizing sacrament for the Church.

The Spiritual Priesthood of Christianity

Many Catholics who are not ordained are surprised to discover that they too are priests. These Catholics have been taught that priesthood is reserved exclusively for those who have a vocation to the ordained ministry. But the Church makes clear in her teaching that a spiritual priesthood is given to all those who are baptized into Jesus Christ.

How so? In the Second Vatican Council's constitution *Lumen Gentium* — which we encountered in the previous chapter — we read:

> Christ the Lord, High Priest taken from among men, made the new people "a kingdom and priests to God the Father." The baptized, by regeneration and the anointing of the Holy Spirit, are consecrated as a spiritual house and a holy priesthood, in order that through all those works which are those of the Christian man they may offer spiritual sacrifices and proclaim the power of Him who has called them out of darkness into His marvelous light. Therefore all the disciples of Christ, persevering in prayer and praising God, should present themselves as a living sacrifice, holy and pleasing to God. Everywhere on earth they must bear witness to Christ and give an answer to those who seek an account of that hope of eternal life which is in them.[1]

Jesus Christ is the great High Priest. In his Incarnation, his death and resurrection, and his Ascension into heaven, he has offered the perfect sacrifice of love to the Father through the instrument of our flesh and blood. This sacrifice of love has created a new people, the Church, now consecrated to God.

Members of the Church participate in a real, spiritual priesthood. To call a newly baptized babe a "priest" is not a pious metaphor. The vocation of that creature is to proclaim, even in his or her infancy, the power of Jesus Christ in the world. That child has a priestly vocation to manifest to his or her parents the reality of divine love, the marvelous light that has enlightened the whole human family through Jesus Christ. The task of each Christian, of whatever age, is to deepen that priesthood through the offering of these spiritual sacrifices. The baptized mom or dad, getting up in the middle of the night to care for an ill child, is not just engaging in an activity natural to parenthood. Mom and dad are consecrating time and space to Christ, caring for an ill child as part of the spiritual sacrifices that all members of the common priesthood are to offer.

The reception of the sacraments, on the part of the faithful, is integral to this spiritual priesthood. The baptized faithful are not passive recipients of the gift of divine love. When the lay faithful come to celebrate the sacrifice of the Eucharist, they are to offer their lives upon that holy altar. When they approach the sacrament of penance, they worship God through confessing their sinfulness, recognizing their incompleteness before the God who is total, self-giving love. In receiving the anointing of the sick, the spiritual priest consecrates his or her illness to God, even if that illness is to end in death itself.

Character and Identity

These are remarkable claims, ones that would likely challenge any baptized person to rethink what it means to belong to the Church. And yet, how is it that the baptized faithful can offer these spiritual sacrifices?

While each of the sacraments of the Church relates to our

identity as men and women united with the God-man, Jesus Christ, there are three sacraments that are especially concerned with the theme of our identity as consecrated to God. Baptism, confirmation, and holy orders are sacraments that may be received no more than once. The reason for this single reception is that these sacraments *fundamentally* change who a person is. They are sacraments that bestow what the Church calls a "character" or "seal." In the *Catechism,* we read:

> The three sacraments of Baptism, Confirmation, and Holy Orders confer, in addition to grace, a sacramental character, or "seal," by which the Christian shares in Christ's priesthood and is made a member of the Church according to different states and functions. This configuration to Christ and to the Church, brought about by the Spirit, is indelible; it remains for ever in the Christian as a positive disposition for grace, a promise and guarantee of divine protection, and as a vocation to divine worship and to the service of the Church. Therefore these sacraments can never be repeated.[2]

Even in the early Church, baptism and confirmation (closely linked to one another as we will see below) were recognized as sacraments that bestowed an indelible mark, or seal, upon the Christian. As the priest and theologian Jean Daniélou remarks about this baptismal seal, "This sacrament is given irrevocably. By sin, a man may withdraw himself from its benefits, but there still endures something that we call the character, whose basis is the irrevocable contract of God's love, officially sealed by the baptismal *sphragis.*"[3] The baptismal *sphragis* — a Greek word meaning "seal" — is the physical signing of the cross on the forehead of the one to be baptized.

The character or seal, therefore, is not some magical power imparted through the Sacraments of Baptism, Confirmation, and Holy Orders. Rather, the character or seal given in these sacraments, the permanent change in identity, is based on the fidelity of God in the sacraments. Human beings cannot cancel out the gift of divine love received in these sacraments, no matter what we do. The character or seal offered in these sacraments relates to God's fidelity more than our own virtue.

Therefore, it is wise to think about character or seal less as an object placed upon the soul, and more as the permanent presence of the God-man, Jesus Christ, in the life of the baptized, confirmed, and ordained person. Matthias Scheeben, in his *Mysteries of Christianity*, makes this point. Sacramental character is a special kind of relationship with Jesus Christ. He writes:

> The nature and significance of the character seem to us to come to this, that it is the signature which makes known that the members of the God-man's mystical body belong to their divine-human head by assimilating them to Him, and testifies to their organic union with Him. ... For to become other Christs, the members must share in the character by which the head becomes Christ. But the signature whereby Christ's humanity receives its divine dignity and consecration is nothing else than its hypostatic union with the Logos. Consequently the character of the members of Christ's mystical body must consist in a seal which establishes and exhibits their relationship to the Logos; their character must be analogous to the hypostatic union and grounded upon it.[4]

At first glance, Scheeben's claim may seem complicated. But let us attend closely to what he is saying. Character is given in the sacraments for the sake of belonging to Jesus Christ. That is the point of character. But belonging to Christ is not reducible to a subjective decision to follow Jesus. Rather, belonging to Christ is to share in his very life. Remember from the first chapter that the sacraments capacitate us to participate in divine life. It's our whole selves that now participate in Jesus' life, death, and resurrection.

This transformation is not a moral task dependent on us. Only God can accomplish it! And God so wants to transform our lives, to transfigure our identity, that there are three sacraments where we are intimately joined to Jesus Christ through receiving the gift of the sacramental character. My identity is changed by God through these sacraments! I am no longer Tim (or Timmy) alone. Rather, it is God himself, through the Spirit, who is now acting through me. Scheeben sees this union as analogous to the hypostatic union. Think back to what we learned about the hypostatic union in the previous chapter. In the language of Scripture, Jesus is the Word or *Logos* made flesh (cf. Jn 1:14). The *Logos*, who is God, has consecrated the humanity of Jesus. The humanity of Jesus Christ was not eclipsed by the *Logos*. Christ's human freedom was not taken away. So too, through the reception of sacramental character, our humanity is transformed in perfect freedom. My identity is no longer exclusively Tim O'Malley, professor of theology, academic administrator par excellence, husband to Kara, and dad to Tommy and Maggie. No! My identity is Christ. None of these other dimensions of my identity are taken away. But now it is Christ who acts in every dimension of my life, who makes it possible for me to offer spiritual sacrifices to the Father through my day-to-day life.

The gift or grace of the sacramental character, therefore, "is an ennobling and elevation of our nature and its activity by their glorification and transformation."[5] This glorification and transformation is Christ now working through us. We participate through the power of the Holy Spirit in Christ's priesthood — in that sacrifice that he offers forever and ever to the Father.

And yet, if the sacramental character is fundamentally about a relationship with Christ, then why are there three sacraments that bestow this character? After all, if Jesus gives himself permanently to us once, do I need to receive him again? Is not baptism sufficient? We will need to look closely at the rites of baptism, confirmation, and holy orders to answer this question.

The Sacraments of Baptism and Confirmation

The Sacraments of Baptism and Confirmation are closely linked in the history of the Church. In the early Church, what we now call the Sacrament of Confirmation was likely a postbaptismal anointing and hand-laying that was given by the bishop in the name of the Father, the Son, and the Holy Spirit.[6] In early medieval Roman Catholicism, the bishop remained the ordinary minister of the Sacrament of Confirmation. But most baptisms were performed upon infants as close as possible to birth. Confirmation would be given later when the bishop could be present in a town or village to confirm anyone who needed the sacrament. In Eastern Christianity, the post-baptismal anointing or confirmation is given not by the bishop normally, but by the priest, so that the newly initiated (even if he or she is an infant) receives all the sacraments of initiation at once: baptism, confirmation, and the Eucharist. Thus, even if baptism and confirmation are separate rites in Roman Catholicism, they must be understood together. The grace, or gift of character, bestowed in these two sacraments are related to one another, and as we will see in the next chapter, are ordered toward full participation in the Eucharistic sacrifice of the Church.

Today, in Roman Catholicism, there are three separate ways to celebrate the Sacraments of Baptism and Confirmation. The *Order of Baptism of Children* is reserved for those children below the age of reason in Catholicism, which is around seven years old. The age of reason is not related to the ability of a child to perform trigonometry or drive a car. Rather, the age of reason is the capacity of the child to distinguish between good and bad, and to recognize the exceptional quality of the Eucharist as heavenly food. The *Order of Baptism of Children* consists of a variety of baptismal rites for children, including a rite for baptizing several children, one child, or many children; a rite to be used by catechists for baptism in the absence of a priest; a rite for baptizing a child in danger of death; and a rite for bringing that child to church for the first time. (The latter is what was once known as the "churching of the child," where mother, father, and baby received a blessing on their first visit to the church).

The second liturgical book for initiation is the *Rite of Christian Initiation for Adults* (RCIA), or more faithfully translated from Latin into English as *The Order of Christian Initiation of Adults* (OCIA).[7] Like the *Order of Baptism of Children*, the RCIA or OCIA consists of a variety of rites, including reception into the catechumenate; rites for celebrating liturgies of the Word of God during the period of the catechumenate; a rite of election to be celebrated by the bishop during Lent; scrutinies for the third, fourth, and fifth Sundays of Lent; and the rites for initiation to be celebrated at the Easter Vigil. Presently, the RCIA or OCIA also includes rites related to the reception of candidates for full communion.[8] (This is for candidates who have already validly received baptism from an ecclesial communion other than Roman Catholicism, and therefore will receive the Sacrament of Confirmation upon entering the Roman Catholic Church.) Reception into full communion is not intended for the Easter Vigil, and for this reason may be celebrated at any other time of year. The minister of confirmation, in this case, is often a priest.

The last liturgical book is the *Order of Celebrating Confirmation*. These rites, including the celebration of confirmation, both during and outside of Mass, are intended primarily for when the bishop celebrates the sacrament. The bishop himself is to confirm all those who are baptized as Catholic before the age of seven. (Even if someone baptized as an infant is ninety-nine when they want to be confirmed, it is the bishop who does the confirmation, because they were first baptized as Catholic.) The bishop remains the ordinary (or normal) celebrant of confirmation in Roman Catholicism, while the priest is the extraordinary (or abnormal, but permissible) celebrant.

What are the signs of both baptism and confirmation, and how are these signs efficacious? The *Catechism* refers to the signs of baptism by recognizing the various names by which this sacrament is called.[9] Baptism is quite literally a "plunging" rite (from the Greek word *baptizein*, which means "to plunge"). One is plunged into the waters, buried with Christ, and then rises with him to new life. Baptism is also a washing and regeneration. Through baptism, one is born into eternal life. The Sacrament of Baptism is both an occasion of death and new birth. This is reflected in the early Church, where baptismal fonts were often in the shape of both a tomb and a womb.[10] Lastly, the Sacrament of Baptism is enlightenment, in which we become sons and daughters who now walk in the light of life.

The *Catechism* quotes a sermon from the Church Father St. Gregory of Nazianzus on these three aspects of baptism:

> Baptism is God's most beautiful and magnificent gift. ...
> We call it gift, grace, anointing, enlightenment, garment
> of immortality, bath of rebirth, seal, and most precious
> gift. It is called *gift* because it is conferred on those who
> bring nothing of their own; *grace* since it is given even
> to the guilty; *Baptism* because sin is buried in the water;
> *anointing* for it is priestly and royal as are those who are
> anointed; *enlightenment* because it radiates light; *cloth-*
> *ing* since it veils our shame; *bath* because it washes; and
> *seal* as it is our guard and the sign of God's Lordship.[11]

Remember what we learned in the last chapter. Sacraments *effect* by signifying. And therefore, the various signs of baptism are all part of this efficaciousness. Baptism washes away sin, burying it in the tomb of water. The postbaptismal anointing with oil transforms us into *Christs* — that is, "anointed ones." That is the literal meaning of the Greek *Christos* — the anointed one. The candle that one receives at baptism is a visible sign of the light that the newly baptized present to the Church and to the world. The newly baptized put on a white garment, signifying their identity as a son or a daughter of the light. Each of these liturgical rites is integral to signifying what takes place within baptism.

The heart of baptism, of course, is the act of the triple immersion into water. In traditional sacramental theology, the water is known as "the matter". The minister of the sacrament says in the Latin West, "N., I baptize you in the name of the Father, and of the Son, and of the Holy Spirit." This is the sacramental form. Dunking someone in water without saying these words is called playing in a pool. Saying these words without water is also insufficient. Both the matter and the form are needed for the sacrament to be both valid and licit. Sacramental validity requires that one perform the rite in the precise way that the Church intends, using the matter and form that the sacraments require. Doing so means the sacraments are valid, and therefore have an effect. Sacramental liceity means that the sacraments have an effect, even if the celebration of the rite is not lawful. A baptism is valid if the person is immersed in the water with the proper formula. A baptism is valid and yet illicit if, for example, a child is secretly baptized by a grandparent who wants the grandchild to be Catholic against the wishes of the parents. In Catholicism, anyone has the authority to baptize — including even, for example, an atheist who decides to do what the Church intends in the sacrament — but a *licit* baptism of an infant or child requires the consent of the parents.

This language, drawn from the Church's legal system (otherwise known as canon law), is intended to guard the heart of the sacramental signs so that they may be effective. After all, why is water so important? As we saw in the last chapter, water is a natural sign that signifies washing, new birth, and the destruction of sin and death. Concurrently, it is a historical sign insofar as God ordered the waters of chaos at creation, led Israel through the waters dry-shod, and gave water from a rock in the desert, while Jesus was baptized in the waters of the river Jordan, and had blood and water pour from his side at his crucifixion.

Further, Jesus Christ himself tells the disciples that they are to go forth and to baptize "in the name of the Father and of the Son and of the Holy Spirit" (Mt 28:19). This is Christ's very command. We are not to baptize in our names or in the name of the community of our parish. The formula of the Church for baptism is to be spoken, because it reflects the divine promise, the gift of love that is to be offered through the Sacrament of Baptism.

One speaks these words not only because Jesus Christ told us to do so. These words are also fitting for what takes place in the sacrament. The Sacrament of Baptism transforms our identity, giving us a new relationship to the God-man Jesus Christ. We are baptized into the name of the Father, the Son, and the Holy Spirit. We may be born as Tim (or Timmy) or Maria to a super nice mom and dad who often have our best interests in mind. But these relationships are always limited. Mom and dad are imperfect; they are creatures just like us. In baptism, we now exist in relationship to the triune God. God is Father, the origin and source of all truth, goodness, and beauty. And yet, his goodness and love are so diffusive that the Father eternally begets a Son. The Son himself reflects the truth, goodness, and beauty of the Father. He gives just like the Father, offering himself in total, self-giving love. The eternal consequence of this love is the

Holy Spirit, the kiss shared between the Father and the Son. In baptism, I now exist in that total, absolute love: *Glory be to the Father, to the Son, and to the Holy Spirit.* As the Church remembers all those moments that God has acted through water, the love of the Spirit descends as a kiss upon those primordial waters of the font. As we are triply immersed in the baptismal womb and tomb, we are taken up into the Father and the Son. We enter, through the power of the Spirit, the very same relationship of love that the Father and the Son share. This relationship of love becomes the central fact of our identity. This is what becoming a Christian means. As Joseph Ratzinger writes:

> Becoming a Christian means sharing in Jesus' prayer, entering into the model provided by his life, that is, the model of his prayer. Becoming a Christian means saying "Father" with Jesus and thus, becoming a child, God's son — God — in the unity of the Spirit, who allows us into the unity of God. Being a Christian means looking at the world from this central point, which gives us freedom, hope, decisiveness, and consolation.[12]

Through baptism, we are now *literally* sons and daughters of the Father by adoption. We are joined to Jesus Christ through baptism. He is the Son of the Father, and we now share in his sonship. When the infant babe is baptized, that infant is anointed with chrism oil, even if he or she is not to be confirmed. This is because that infant is now a little *Christ*. Baptized into Christ, this little creature shares in the priesthood of Jesus, not because he or she has earned it, but as sheer gift.[13]

The gift of baptism, the grace of this new identity, remains true whether we are talking about infant or adult baptism. Baptism is a sacrament of faith, but it is not a sacrament where an individual proves him- or herself worthy of baptism through exhibiting an individualized and perfected faith. In infant baptism, the faith that is relied upon is the faith of the entire communion of believers as made manifest in the faith of parents and godparents. In adult baptism, the candidate for baptism may be better able to express his or her personal relationship with Jesus Christ, and yet the adult still relies on the faith of the Church, rather than on his or her own "earned" faith. After all, where does the Creed come from? It is not the product of an individualized faith, but has been received by the catechumen as a gift from a history, a tradition, and a community of men and women who have passed faith onto us.

The effects of baptism are all related to this character, or seal, that allows us to be united to the person of Jesus Christ. Baptism forgives, or washes away, both original and actual sin. Original sin is the loss of the original holiness that God intended for every man and woman. There is something about the human person that is off, a bit strange. Original sin is a state of being and not a moral fault. We are born as human creatures who tend to reject love, and yet God intended at creation something more for each of us. Actual sin is our culpability, the decisions we have consciously made (whether by commission or omission) to reject God's love. When we are baptized into the name of the Father, the Son, and the Holy Spirit, both kinds of sin are forgiven. The character that we receive in baptism now orders us toward the self-giving love of the Word made flesh. Original and actual sin are wiped away through the cleansing waters of baptism.

For adults, the problem of sin is very different than for an infant. An infant may be oriented toward sinfulness, lacking the original holiness that God intended, but an adult has actively sinned. For this reason, the RCIA or OCIA is a process of learning to desire holiness rather than sin. That is why one does not just work with an adult for three weeks, teach them key passages in the *Catechism*, and then baptize them immediately. Rather, the process of formation is a kind of conversion therapy, whereby the adult learns what it means to say that Jesus Christ is the meaning of their life through the community of the Church. This takes time, often at least a year or two.

But even in the case of an adult who may consciously choose to enter the Church, this washing away of sin is only the beginning. The purpose of the forgiveness is to make us "'a new creature,' an adopted son of God, who has become a 'partaker of the divine nature,' member of Christ and co-heir with him, and a temple of the Holy Spirit."[14] The *telos*, or end, of baptism is not just saving one from sin and death, from the powers of hell, but true sanctification through communion with Christ. We are to become like God, to become divine. An infant can experience this communion as much as an adult. What dignity there is in baptism, that all creatures, no matter their age, no matter their socioeconomic status, no matter their race, may become, through baptism, sons and daughters of the living God!

The Sacrament of Baptism initiates one into the communion of the Church. The newly baptized are now members of a common priesthood. Jesus Christ is the great High Priest, who continually offers himself in perfect love to the Father. To be the Son is to be for others, to treat existence as a gift.

In the Church, baptism brings us into relationships that transcend biological necessity. The infant babe is ordered by nature to love mother and father. But the baptized child or the newly initiated adult (what the Church calls a neophyte, or the "newly born") has received as a gift a relationship with the visible and invisible Church that transcends biological necessity. The newly baptized has brothers and sisters in a parish community who are not blood relatives. The neophytes are in relationship with the whole communion of saints, living and dead. Each of the baptized are to live for the sanctification of human life, rather than their own well-being alone. Salvation, in Catholicism, is a personal, albeit not individual, affair. I am saved and sanctified, not apart from but in communion with, the unity of the Church.

Consequently, the character that I have received through baptism is not given exclusively for my own individual sanctification. My relationship with Christ, my identity as a son or daughter of God, is meant for the communion of the whole world. I have been given my priesthood for the consecration of all things to Christ.

Baptism, as you can see, is a remarkable sacrament. Why, then, is there a need for another sacramental character beyond that of union with Christ? Here, we approach the thorny problem of confirmation, a dilemma that we ourselves created.[15] Until Pope Saint Pius X lowered the age of first holy Communion to seven years of age, confirmation was received before first Communion. Pius X had intended for confirmation still to be received before first Communion, but most dioceses throughout the world did not adjust the age of confirmation. For this reason, confirmation in the United States may be bestowed on baptized Catholics anywhere between the ages of seven years through late adolescence.

The shifting age of confirmation has led some theologians and catechists to reinterpret it as an adolescent rite of passage. How many times have you heard a catechist say that confirmation is when a Catholic makes her faith her own? It is the moment when one becomes an "adult" Christian.

There is some good warrant to treat confirmation as a sacrament of maturation or perfection. The *Catechism of the Catholic Church* describes the effects of confirmation as a deepening of baptismal grace through a fresh outpouring of the Holy Spirit. Against the traditional theology of the sacrament, much of the twentieth-century account of confirmation has made the sacrament primarily about us. How do *we* as Catholics make *our* faith *our* own? This is a question that any maturing Christian must answer. And yet, the Sacrament of Confirmation is not dependent on our appropriation of Catholicism. The Sacrament of Confirmation must describe what God is doing in the sacrament, not how we are earning it.

And what is God doing in confirmation? Here, one must turn to the signs of confirmation proper. The sign of confirmation (or what the Christian East calls Chrismation) is the consecrated oil of chrism. In the ancient world, oil signified abundance, cleansing, loosening of the limbs (athletes used it), soothing and healing, and even making the human face radiant with glory.[16] This same oil in the Old Testament was used to anoint kings. In the New Testament, Jesus is the *Christ,* the Anointed One upon whom the Spirit descends in the waters of the Jordan. The apostles are also anointed by the same Spirit on Pentecost, sent forth like Christ on mission to the end of the world. In addition, confirmation in the early Church included the imposition of hands. To impose hands upon someone is to bestow on them an office, a specific mission in the world.

Confirmation, therefore, is a sacrament that deepens the baptismal identity of the Christian. It is a totalizing consecration of the Christian. As the *Catechism* notes:

> The post-baptismal anointing with sacred chrism in Confirmation and ordination is the sign of consecration. By Confirmation Christians, that is, those who are anointed, share more completely in the mission of Jesus Christ and the fullness of the Holy Spirit with which he is filled, so that their lives may give off "the aroma of Christ."[17]

The newly baptized receives a new identity as a son or daughter of the living God. This identity comes with a call or vocation to unite ourselves completely with the mission of Jesus Christ. This is not something that we can do on our own. "What Would Jesus Do" is a nice sentiment. But let us remember that Jesus is the Word made flesh, the splendor of the Father, the one who loved his own until the bitter end. We are to become witnesses to the divine love that we first received.

The Sacrament of Confirmation or Chrismation is the gift of the Spirit that orients us toward mission. In the case of an Eastern Christian, chrismation takes place immediately after baptism. Let us remember, the infant is consecrated unto God in baptism and may then participate in the charism, or gift, of consecration that is confirmation. Confirmation, in some dioceses, takes place before first reception of holy Communion. This restored order — returning the sacraments of initiation to their original and theological order of baptism, confirmation, and Eucharist — presumes that confirmation is about a perfect participation in the mission of Christ. The sacrament is given in its fullness, regardless of the age of the recipient. There is no reason that a seven-year-old cannot participate in the mission of Jesus Christ, to become a living witness of love unto the end. In confirmation, baptismal promises are renewed. The bishop extends his hands over those to be confirmed, and prays for a new outpouring of the Spirit. The seven-year-old, for example, is anointed with chrism on the forehead, and the bishop says, "Be sealed with the Gift of the Holy Spirit." The chrism is the matter of the sacrament, while these words are the form. Lastly, a sign of peace is shared between the bishop and the faithful. The same rite is celebrated with adolescents or adults who participate in the Sacrament of Confirmation after they receive their first holy Communion.

The Latin West recognizes that confirmation may be celebrated either at the age of the restored order, or later in life after first holy Communion. If both ways of celebrating are acceptable to the Church, then we must recognize the evangelizing potential in both. A seven-year-old, acknowledging that he has a mission from Christ, may be an evangelizing influence for his mother and father and for his neighborhood. At the same time, an adolescent — who is in a stage of physical, spiritual, and social maturation — may discover in the Sacrament of Confirmation a new outpouring of the Spirit that sends her out on a mission to publicly profess Christ to the world.

In any case, confirmation deepens and perfects the consecration of baptism. The character that is given in confirmation is not separate from the character of baptism, but is best understood as perfective. It "confirms" and thus deepens the already existing, objective relationship with Jesus Christ that defines the identity of the baptized person. The spiritual sacrifice that each Christian is to offer may become a perfect sacrifice. In the restored order, confirmation culminates — even if first Communion is celebrated a year later, as it is in some dioceses — in the perfect sacrifice of the Eucharist. Once confirmed, the child receives Christ's Body and Blood, entering more fully into union with Christ and the Church. When confirmation is celebrated after first Communion, the sacrament is still ideally celebrated in the context of the Eucharistic liturgy.

Holy Orders

Most accounts of the sacraments treat holy orders under the sacraments of vocation, rather than sacraments that bestow character. One problem with this is that holy orders is separated from both baptism and confirmation. Keep in mind that the Sacrament of Holy Orders is bestowed for the sake of the spiritual sacrifices of all the faithful in the Church.

The history of the Sacrament of Holy Orders is somewhat complicated. Indeed, the early Church did not possess the same, clear account of sacramental ministry that we do today. This does not mean that holy orders is therefore a later interpolation disconnected from the will of Christ.[18] As Jean-Pierre Torrell, a Catholic theologian and priest, writes:

> [I]f it is clear that Christ did not found the episcopacy and the presbyterate as we know them today, it is nevertheless his will that lay at the root of the sending of the apostles and of the measures taken by them with the authority with which he entrusted them so that their mission could be pursued in the Holy Spirit, who also gave them authority.[19]

Human actors were involved in the formation of the Church's theology of the bishop, the priest, and the deacon. Confessing this does not mean that this development is a mere accident of history. Rather, the Spirit often works through historical, and thus human, developments.

Importantly, the *Catechism* discusses holy orders in the context of a twofold priesthood of the Christian life. Baptism and confirmation are moments of consecration to the common priesthood of the faithful. Holy orders, in fact, depends on the reception of this common priesthood by the one being ordained. A priest is not someone who has graduated from baptized life, leaving it behind for clerical power. It is only through baptism that the gift of order is possible at all. As the *Catechism* clarifies:

> The ministerial or hierarchical priesthood of bishops and priests, and the common priesthood of all the faithful participate, "each in its own proper way, in the one priesthood of Christ." While being "ordered one to another," they differ essentially. ... While the common priesthood of the faithful is exercised by the unfolding of baptismal grace ... the ministerial priesthood is at the service of the common priesthood. It is directed at the

unfolding of the baptismal grace of all Christians. The ministerial priesthood is a *means* by which Christ unceasingly builds up and leads his Church.[20]

Holy orders is therefore a call that a man receives not exclusively for his own well-being, but for the benefit of the priesthood of the baptized. His identity is ordered toward cultivating the communion of the common priesthood through teaching, governing, and celebrating the sacraments.

This chapter cannot address every theological nuance related to holy orders. Holy orders, as a sacrament, has three degrees including the diaconate, the priesthood, and the episcopacy. While each are ordinations, according to Church teaching, only the episcopacy and the presbyterate are strictly speaking a "ministerial participation in the priesthood of Christ."[21] The diaconate is ordered toward the service of that ministerial priesthood. It is for this reason that the question of the female diaconate is presently under discussion in Rome.[22] In any case, deacons, priests, and bishops each receive a sacramental character.

This character is given for the sake of the baptized faithful. No human being can make the gift of divine love available on his or her own. The bishop, priest, and deacon are often fallible (and sometimes, as we have painfully relearned in our day, a sinner of the highest order). For this reason, a sacrament is given by the Church to this man so that he may represent that which he is otherwise incapable of representing — the God-man, Jesus Christ.

Think about the Eucharist. At every Mass, the priest speaks the words of Institution. Jesus Christ said at the Last Supper that "This is my Body" and "This is my Blood." How can a priest say these words? How can these words, said by a mere mortal, bring about the Eucharistic presence of our Lord?

Unto himself, a priest cannot say these words and transform

bread and wine into the Body and Blood of Christ. But through the Sacrament of Holy Orders, it is no longer he who acts, but Christ in him. Likely, you have heard that the priest at Mass acts *in persona Christi Capitis* — in the person of Christ the Head. Through the Sacrament of Holy Orders, the priest becomes the living instrument of Christ acting among us. Once again, this is not because the priest is a good person, especially worthy of this gift. Rather, like baptism, it is a sacramental gift, a grace bestowed for the whole Church. The priest receives the character to act in the person of Christ the Head. The sacraments are given to the faithful, therefore, not because the individual minister is always faithful himself to the covenant, but because God is faithful through the identity of the ordained ministry.

The liturgy of each degree of order is linked to that of God's way of giving. At the heart of the liturgy is the laying on of hands by the bishop on the head of the ordinand. This is the matter of the sacrament. The bishop prays for the outpouring of the Spirit on the ordinand using a consecratory prayer (which is the sacramental form of each respective order) and hands over the instruments of the office. For a deacon, it is the Book of the Gospels. For a priest, it is the paten and chalice. For a bishop, it is the Gospels, the ring, the miter, and the crosier. The gift that is bestowed in the sacrament, the character that is given, is relational. The bishop's identity is changed for the sake of the people; he is given the sacred duty to govern as Christ. The priest is ordained for the sake of offering the Eucharistic Sacrifice for the Church as Christ. The deacon is ordained to become a servant of the Gospel as Christ.

Holy orders, in Catholicism, is reserved for men. This is not because the Catholic Church requires a male-only priesthood. Remember that the common priesthood is a real, authentic priesthood that consecrates the entire world to God. Women and non-ordained men throughout the world are exercising this priesthood even as you are reading this chapter. It is true to say that the Catholic Church reserves the ministerial or hierarchical priesthood to men. The *Catechism* notes that this is the case because Christ chose men as the twelve apostles. The male priesthood, according to the teaching of the Church (though some theologians disagree), is not simply an accident of history. After all, Jesus has women, including Mary Magdalene, involved in ministry in all sorts of ways in the New Testament. The ministerial priesthood — closely connected to the Apostles — is to be understood as a specific mission to represent Christ as Redeemer within the sacramental life of the Church for the sake of the common priesthood.[23]

Sister Sara Butler, a theologian who has written on the priesthood and masculinity, notes that the sacramental sign itself of the male body is especially fitting for the Church. She writes:

> Because the scriptures depict God and Christ in the role of the Bridegroom, a role exclusive to men, it is fitting for a man to be the sacramental sign of Christ, who was and remains a man, in this relationship. The priest acts in the person of the Bridegroom with respect to the Bride-Church in the celebration of the sacrament of the New Covenant.[24]

This may be a controversial claim for many of us today. Does the sex of the ordained minister matter? Not a few theologians reject Butler's nuptial or bridal imagery of the Church, because they presume that it leads to misogyny. Men have all the power as Bridegroom, but women possess nothing. Yet, this is to misunderstand how nuptial imagery functions in the Bible. The Bridegroom demonstrates power not through force or violence, but through self-emptying love. The priest, who acts in the person of Christ and the Church in the Eucharist, is representing that Bridegroom in the sacrament. As a baptized person, he is a member of the Church called to preside over the Eucharistic Liturgy. As ordained, he is to become the image of Christ the Bridegroom in the Eucharist. That is who he is, and his identity as a man matters in the act of signification. Remember our principle: Sacraments effect by signifying.

For this reason, the Sacrament of Holy Orders (for bishop, priest, or deacon) is always an invitation to conversion. If you are to represent Christ the Head in the Eucharistic Sacrifice, then you must become like Christ the Head. What is given in the sacrament is a new identity. A bishop, priest, or deacon who abuses his authority does not have that identity taken away from him — for the sake of the common priesthood of believers, who are reliant on the efficacy of his sacramental ministry — but he is nonetheless living a lie. Sure, a bad priest can give homilies, govern a parish, and celebrate the Sacrament of the Eucharist. Many of these things may benefit the whole Church, even if he is a bad person. When he administers the sacraments, infants are really baptized and the Eucharist is really celebrated. But even though sacramental grace is effected through his ministry, such a priest fails to live up to the identity that he has received through the Sacrament of Holy Orders.

This failure of some priests to live up to their sacramental identity in holy orders is an obstacle to evangelization today. The gift of divine life, or grace, that is given in the Sacrament of Holy Orders is connected to the concrete ministry that the bishop, priest, or deacon performs. Concluding with a line from Father Jean-Pierre Torrell, holy orders "is not enough to give the person who receives [grace] a greater holiness. The grace is destined to help the person better fulfill his ministry; fidelity to that grace will permit him to acquire that increase in holiness by the very carrying out of its assignment."[25] And that assignment is not about personal power, but total, self-giving love and service to the priesthood of the baptized.

All the sacraments that bestow character are ordered to this Eucharistic charity, to the spiritual sacrifices that the human family is to offer in Jesus Christ. And it is for this reason that we turn to the Sacrament of the Eucharist in the next chapter. The Eucharist is that most evangelizing of all the sacraments.

Chapter 3

The Eucharist and the
Sacrifice of Time

In the first chapter, we learned that the sacraments function analogically with physical growth. Through baptism and confirmation, we are reborn as sons and daughters of the living God. And yet, those who are born also need nourishment to grow. For St. Thomas Aquinas, the Eucharist is the privileged sacrament of nourishment for growth in the spiritual life.

We also discovered in the second chapter that baptism, confirmation, and holy orders bring about a fundamental change in identity. In baptism and confirmation, we receive a character, or seal, that orders us toward making a spiritual sacrifice with our lives in the Church. And thus, every Catholic finds the fulfillment of his or her vocation in the sacrificial worship of the Eucharist.

In this third chapter, we look to the Sacrament of the Eucharist as both nourishing us and enabling us to fulfill our vocation as those who have been made to adore the living God. The Sacrament of the Eucharist is that sacrificial food which makes present, through the power of the Holy Spirit and the Church's prayer, the Body and Blood of Christ. The Eucharist is a sacrificial meal by which we are nourished to become ever more sons and daughters of the living God, exercising our baptismal priesthood. This transformation takes place as we dwell together in the Church in time. If we are careful to attend to the various "times" of the Eucharist — the past, the present, and the future — we receive insight into what it means to live a life in Christ in history.

St. Thomas Aquinas on Eucharistic Time

Likely, all those who have studied the Sacrament of the Eucharist have heard of St. Thomas Aquinas. He not only wrote about the Eucharist in his two works, the *Summa Contra Gentiles* and the *Summa Theologiae*, but he is also the author of the Latin texts for the feast of Corpus Christi. If you have sung in your parish *Adoro Te Devote* or the *Tantum Ergo* (the last two stanzas of the *Pange Lingua*), you are familiar with some of Saint Thomas's Eucharistic theology.[1]

In the fourth article of question 73 of the *Summa Theologiae*, Saint Thomas carefully defines what constitutes the Sacrament of the Eucharist by attending to its various names.[2] According to Saint Thomas, the Eucharist has a three-fold temporal significance — the Eucharist refers to the past, the present, and the future. According to the past, the Eucharist is Christ's sacrifice. In the present, it is Communion, because through the Eucharist we partake of the Flesh and Blood of Jesus Christ. In the future, it refers to the fullness of grace that we will enjoy in heaven, or the beatific vision itself — when we will see God face-to-face.

This movement between past, present, and future is important to the Sacrament of the Eucharist in particular. Remember that the definition of a sacrament, which we treated in the first chapter, depends on careful attention to the specifics of the efficacious signs of that sacrament. The Eucharist is a weird sacrament when compared to baptism or confirmation. In baptism and confirmation, Christ acts in the sacrament through the signs. The water of baptism remains water. Consecrated oil, although sacred, remains oil, and is not the Flesh and Blood of Jesus. But in the Eucharist, Christ himself becomes substantially present in the species, or appearances, of bread and wine. We genuflect before the tabernacle in a way that we would never genuflect before consecrated oils. This is because the One who created the world out of love, who redeemed Israel, who died upon the cross and rose again, and who is now seated in heaven, is made really, or substantially, present among us through the sacrament. We are present before the resurrected and glorified Lord in the sacrament.

For this reason, Saint Thomas returns to the question of time in the sixth article of question 73. This time (sorry for the pun), Saint Thomas asks whether the Paschal Lamb of Exodus is the chief or primary figure (here, "figure" refers to "an image that points toward") of the sacrament. He answers "yes," but his "yes" comes with distinctions. As any reader of St. Thomas Aquinas knows, good theology always involves distinctions. For Saint Thomas, we can consider three things when we analyze any sacrament. The first is the *sacramentum tantum*, or the "sign alone." In the Eucharist, the sign itself is the sacrifice of bread and wine presented on the altar. If we are considering the Eucharist as bread and wine, the principal figure of the sacrament is Melchizedek, the mysterious Old Testament king in Genesis who offered a sacrifice of bread and wine. The second thing we can consider is the *sacramentum et res*, or the "sign and the reality (or thing) together." The *sacramentum et res* is Christ's true Body, given over in the Eucharist. The chief figure here is Christ crucified. The final thing we can consider is the *res tantum*, or the "reality (or thing) itself." This is the effect of the sacrament. The Eucharistic *res tantum* is the grace that refreshes the soul of the believer, which unites us more closely to the Church. The figure of this sacrament is manna, the bread from heaven, that is given to Israel in the Book of Exodus.

For Saint Thomas, the perfect figure, or image, of the Eucharist in the Old Testament is the Paschal Lamb. The Paschal Lamb is food, eaten with unleavened bread. The bread and wine (the *sacramentum tantum*) of the Eucharist are foretold through the Passover. They refer to the history of Israel, to the way that God has redeemed his people in the past. At the same time, the Paschal Lamb is sacrificed. The lamb is truly slain; its life is given to be consumed. So too in the Eucharist, we receive the true Body of Jesus Christ (what we earlier referred to as the *sacramentum et res*). This is what we refer to as the Real Presence of Christ in the Eucharist. Lastly, the Eucharist points toward the promised land, where all of Israel will dwell together in unity, worshiping God and loving neighbor. The sweet grace of the Eucharist (the *res tantum*) is foretold in the liberation of Israel from sin and death and Israel's entrance into perfect freedom. The perfect charity made possible by God's gift, the freedom to love, is something that is not entirely available in the present, but points the Church toward the future. After all, Israel wanders in the desert for years before the people enter the promised land. Saint Thomas's interpretation of the Old Testament and the Eucharist includes a union of past, present, and future.

This union of past, present, and future is integral if we want to understand why the Sacrament of the Eucharist is so essential to Catholic life. In the previous chapter, we looked at the question of identity. What does it mean to have an identity? Part of possessing an identity is knowing who we are. We are those who are baptized into Jesus Christ, sealed with the gift of the Spirit. I am a priest, a prophet, and a king, called to offer the entire world back to God.

But knowing who one is remains only one part of cultivating an identity. An identity is also linked to our ability to understand who we are across time. What is my past, and how has it shaped me? What is the meaning of my life here and now? What is my future, and what shall I become? Although these questions are normally reserved for periods of adolescence or emerging adulthood, a reflective person often finds him or herself asking these questions throughout life.

The Eucharist is a privileged place where we not only ask these questions, but we ask them in the context of worshiping in the presence of the living God. The Eucharist as a sacrament forms us to see our lives — past, present, and future — as a gift, and to offer this gift of our lives back to God. The fundamental Christian vocation, or calling, according to the sacraments, is the Eucharist.[3]

The Eucharistic Past: The Sacrifice of Christ

St. Thomas Aquinas composed an antiphon for the feast of Corpus Christi that has often been set to music. The antiphon is O Sacrum Convivium, and it states:

O sacrum convivium!
in quo Christus sumitur:
recolitur memoria passionis eius:
mens impletur gratia:
et futurae gloriae nobis pignus datur.
Alleluia.

O sacred banquet!

In which Christ is consumed:
the memory of his passion is recalled:
the mind is filled with grace:
and a pledge of future glory is given.
Alleluia.

In the antiphon, notice that when we eat Christ's Body and Blood, we are recalling the memory of his Passion. How can an act of eating also be an act of recollection or remembering?

Here, it is important to understand what the Church means by "memory." If I exhort you to remember the founding of the United States of America, you would likely recall what you have learned about Paul Revere, the Declaration of Independence, the Revolutionary War, and maybe even the musical *Hamilton*. In remembering each of these occurrences, you would not suddenly find yourself present at the signing of the Declaration of Independence, or immersed in the Battle of Yorktown. The signing of the Declaration, and the Battle of Yorktown, are in the past, and you are not. Sure, you could go to a costume shop, buy an American Revolutionary soldier's uniform, and set your backyard up like Yorktown, but you would still not be "present" to the founding events. At best, you would be playacting.

The Church, however, operates out of a unique and distinct sense of memory, one in which the act of remembering what God has done in the past makes the past event present to us. As the *Catechism* declares:

> Christian liturgy not only recalls the events that saved us but actualizes them, makes them present. The Paschal mystery of Christ is celebrated, not repeated. It is the celebrations that are repeated, and in each celebration there is an outpouring of the Holy Spirit that makes the unique mystery present.[4]

Each Christmas, as we remember that the Word became flesh, a babbling babe in Bethlehem, the saving event of the Incarnation becomes present to us. The same is true in each of the sacraments. As the penitent listens to the Word of God, confessing his or her sins, it is the merciful forgiveness of Christ the Healer who is made present in the moment. The Church calls this kind of remembering *anamnesis*. It is a word, in Greek, that refers to a kind of remembering that is not just a recollection, but a participation in the remembered event.

The Church "remembers" the passion of Christ in the Eucharist through the signs of unleavened bread and wine (the matter of the Eucharist), together with the words of Institution (the form of the Eucharist). Bread and wine represent the Sacrifice of Christ as both natural and historical signs. Bread is made through wheat that is ground down, formed into one loaf, and then baked upon a fire. Wine comes about through a process of crushing grapes and fermentation, which creates a liquid that gladdens our hearts. Historically, bread and wine refer to a variety of sacrifices made in the Scriptures. The mysterious Gentile priest Melchizedek offers bread and wine. Bread and wine are central to the Passover sacrifice in Exodus. And bread is given from heaven as manna to Israel in the desert, as they learn to trust in God.

In the New Testament, Jesus Christ, on the night before he died, shared a Passover (or Passover-themed) meal with his disciples.[5] The Pauline account of the institution narrative from this meal is a window into the early meaning of the Eucharist for Christians:

> For I received from the Lord what I also delivered to you, that the Lord Jesus on the night when he was betrayed took bread, and when he had given thanks, he broke it, and said, "This is my body which is for you. Do this in

remembrance of me." In the same way also the chalice, after supper, saying, "This chalice is the new covenant in my blood. Do this, as often as you drink it, in remembrance of me." For as often as you eat this bread and drink the chalice, you proclaim the Lord's death until he comes. (1 Corinthians 11:23–26)

The bread is his Body. The wine is his Blood. In eating and drinking the Eucharist, the Christian is showing forth the Lord's death until he comes again. A present act of eating makes present a past event.

This is because the Lord's death and resurrection, as we saw in the first chapter, is still operative. The Sacrifice of Christ, though offered once and for all, is in the prayer of the Church today because of the Paschal Mystery of Jesus Christ. In a short work titled *The Eucharist: Heart of the Church*, Joseph Ratzinger writes about the presence of this sacrifice:

> The Last Supper alone is not sufficient for the institution of the Eucharist. For the words that Jesus spoke then are an anticipation of his death, a transformation of his death into an event of love, a transformation of what is meaningless into something that is significant. … But that also means that these words carry weight and have creative power for all time only in that they did not remain mere words but were given content by his actual death. … The death [itself] would remain empty of meaning, and would also render the words meaningless, if the Resurrection had not come about, whereby it is made clear that these words were spoken with divine authority, that his love is indeed strong enough to reach out beyond death.[6]

The Sacrifice of the Last Supper is an act where Jesus Christ takes up his death, transforming it into an offering. He gives his Body. He gives his Blood. The God-man takes the darkness of death, making it into a sacrifice of love. Sacrifice is not, in this case, violence. It is rather love unto the end, transfigured through the prayer that the Son offers to the Father on the cross. This sacrifice of love is accepted in the Resurrection and Ascension, our very human flesh and blood now dwelling at the right hand of the Father.

The Eucharist is the answer to a question that gnaws at the soul of any attentive human being. Not just "Why does a person suffer in general?" or "Why might I suffer in the future?" but "Why *did* I suffer?" In the Sacrifice of Christ, made available in the Eucharist through the signs of what look like bread and wine, we receive from God not an explanation, but the gift of love. Suffering can be transformed through the love of the Word made flesh. Death is not the end; love is stronger, and divine love can transform every dimension of human love — even the darkness — into a sacrifice of love. *This is my Body. This is my Blood.* Past suffering, both personal and historical, is transformed through the love of God made present in the Eucharist.

This, of course, is why the Sacrifice of the Mass is evangelizing, whether anyone is aware of it or not. The Sacrifice is an act of love offered to the Father. My corner of the world is transfigured through the Eucharistic offering of Christ, celebrated every day by a priest in my local parish. It is better for people to understand what is happening in the Mass, longing to participate in it. But the celebration of Mass is invaluable in itself — even if those attending it are not attuned to what Mass really entails, and even if they are only attending it out of a sense of duty and would rather not even be there. The celebration of the Mass is in itself evangelizing, as every corner of the cosmos becomes a space where Christ's sacrificial love is offered. Even during

COVID-19, Mass was not canceled. It was celebrated by many priests. The Sacrifice remained available, present to the Church and the world.

This Sacrifice, of course, is not just offered by Jesus at Mass, but is also offered by his Body, the Church. The words of the Eucharistic Prayer prayed by the priest, in the name of the Church, is a return gift of love offered back to the Father. Again, turning to Ratzinger, "By putting these words into our mouths, letting us pronounce them with him, he permits us and enables us to make the offering with him: his words become our words, his worship our worship, his sacrifice our sacrifice."[7] Is this not the precise nourishment that every maturing Christian needs? We are not meant to be passive spectators of a sacrifice that happened once upon a time. Rather, we are to let our sacrifice of praise be transformed by the words of Christ through the Eucharist. He longs to speak his Word, his *Logos,* through our very words.

The Eucharistic Present: The Grace of Presence

The strangeness of the Eucharist, as we have already seen, is that the past Sacrifice of Christ is made present to us now. The past has become the present. And yet, St. Thomas Aquinas, in his antiphon for Corpus Christi, also says that the mind is filled with grace as we presently eat and drink the Body and Blood of Christ.

Catholics teach that the Eucharist is the Real Presence of Christ.[8] Real Presence, as a term, does not mean that Christ is not *really* present in the Sacrament of Baptism, in the Scriptures, or in the hungry and thirsty. Rather, it is best to think about the Eucharist as a *unique* presence of Christ made possible through the substantial transformation of bread and wine into the Body and Blood of Christ.

This conversion of bread and wine into the Body and Blood of Christ is what the Church means by transubstantiation. Bread and wine, like everything, have "substances." We think about substance as the "stuff" that makes something what it is. The substance of my computer is polished glass and microchips. Therefore, the substance of bread and wine would be wheat and grapes, respectively. And the substance of Christ's Body would be his flesh and bones.

But we need to keep in mind that the Church adopted the language of "substance" from Aristotle, not from contemporary science. Substance is not the same as the collection of matter in a thing, because substance is not visible. Substance is the fundamental identity of a thing that makes that thing what it is at the level of identity. For example, my daughter sees four dogs. One is tall, the other short, one is fat, and the other skinny. The dogs are all different colors. And yet, my daughter can joyfully exclaim when she sees each dog, "Hey, a doggie." Through attending to the "accidents" (or physical attributes of the creature), she is able to come to a recognition of its invisible identity — that it is a dog; not even just any dog, but my dog.[9]

In transubstantiation, the substances of bread and wine become the Body and Blood of Jesus Christ. There is no more bread and wine there. And yet, the species, or accidents, of bread and wine remain, through a miracle. God sustains the accidents of bread and wine, even if there is no substance attached to them.

Like many in the Church today, your initial reaction to this account of Eucharistic conversion may be to roll your eyes. Is it necessary to use so much technical language in explaining Christ's presence in the sacrament? Could we not simply remain silent before the mystery of presence?

But that is to make a fundamental mistake. The doctrine of transubstantiation exists so that we may better delight in the mystery of the Eucharist. In the aftermath of the Protestant Reformation, the Council of Trent (1545–63) taught transubstantiation as the most apt way of describing the Eucharistic mystery precisely because it expressed what it means to eat and drink the Body and Blood of Christ under the signs of bread and wine.[10] In what looks like bread and wine, Jesus Christ gives the completeness of himself to us. He becomes truly present to us. But the conversion described by transubstantiation is not abhorrent to our sensibilities. An overly physicalist interpretation of the Eucharist would say that Jesus' bones are hidden in what looks like bread and wine. When we chew on the Host, we would be chewing on these flesh and bones. But that is not what the doctrine of transubstantiation says. Christ becomes present in substance, in that which is not perceptible to the senses. It is the fullness of the God-man, who dwells among us within the Church. And yet, the species remain so that we may enter into an intimate union with Christ in a way that is appropriate to a human being. We eat bread and wine, while only cannibals eat flesh and blood.

In fact, we are not really the ones who are eating Christ at all. Rather, in our act of eating, we are consumed by the presence of Christ. The Real Presence is not a technical explanation of the Eucharist as much as it is a way of describing how we are united substantially with Jesus Christ through eating what looks like bread and wine. Matthias Scheeben, in his account of the Real Presence, describes this union: "Bread is changed into the body of him who eats it. But Christ, who is incapable of such change, takes the partaker to Himself, not by transforming his substance, but by joining him substantially to Himself as a member that belongs to Him and is to be animated by Him."[11] Remember what we said in chapter two. In baptism, the Christian is joined to the person of the Son. In eating and drinking the Body and Blood of Christ — who is immersing us in his divine love — there is a deepening of this union.

There are other theories of the Eucharistic Presence that have been offered — and all have problems from a Roman Catholic perspective, if they are the primary way in which the Eucharist is approached. One is transignification, in which the Eucharist is changed, not at the level of substance, but meaning. The bread and the wine no longer mean the same thing after we speak the words of Institution. At one level, this is true. Bread and wine do change their meaning when the words of Institution are spoken. But they change their meaning because they change what they are substantially. The bread and wine are no longer there, and if we suddenly said new words over them, the bread and wine would not revert to what they were. There is an objective, sacramental change.

Likewise, some Protestants and Catholics propose consubstantiation. Here, the substances of bread and wine exist alongside the Body and Blood of Christ. The problem with consubstantiation is that we do not treat the Eucharist as if there are two separate substances. We adore the Eucharist as the personal and sacramental Presence of Christ, as evidenced by the many Latino and Latina Catholics who proclaim during the consecration, in the words of St. Thomas the Apostle, "My Lord and my God." Of course, the signs of bread and wine still matter. The species or accidents remain, sustained through a miracle. But they are intended to feed us with the Presence of Christ.

Real Presence, therefore, is at the heart of the Sacrament of the Eucharist, because it is a doctrine that deals with the intimate, loving presence of the God-man to the Church. The Eucharist is not an object to be schlepped around. Rather, the Eucharist is the personal and sacramental Presence of Christ, fully given to us in what looks like bread and wine. We bend our knee before the Eucharist, sing hymns of praise to the Host, examine ourselves before approaching Communion, remain silent after eating and drinking the Body and Blood of Christ, and keep vigil over the tabernacle, because it is the Lord who is there.

All of this is known exclusively through faith. We cannot perceive the substantial conversion of bread and wine into Body and Blood in the Eucharist. Analogously, the maturing Christian cannot always recognize the intimate union of Christ that is transforming his or her history. Life happens, and it is not always wonderful. And yet, even in the darkest hour, Christ is there.

The Eucharistic Future

Sometimes Catholics focus so much on the Eucharistic Sacrifice and Presence that we forget that the Eucharist is also a pledge of future glory. Through the Eucharist, we receive a foretaste of eternal life with God, and begin to participate in the gift of divine life offered by Christ. As Saint Thomas concludes in his Eucharistic hymn *Adoro Te Devote*, "Jesus, whom now I see hidden/I ask you to fulfill what I so desire: That the sight of Your Face being unveiled/I may have the happiness of seeing your glory." Through the Sacrament of the Eucharist, the Catholic is taught to see beyond what is immediately perceivable, to long for the fullness of redemption revealed in Christ.

What, after all, are the fruits of Eucharistic communion according to the *Catechism*?[12] First, we are united more closely to Jesus Christ, who nourishes us with his presence. Second, we are cleansed of sin, the virtue of love is enflamed in our hearts, and we are protected from future mortal sin — those serious sins that cut us off from communion with Christ and the Church. Third, we are wedded more closely to the Church as the mystical Body of Christ. Remember from our previous chapter — baptism and confirmation are not just about us, but belonging to the whole communion of believers. Fourth, we are committed to give ourselves more fully to those who are poor. Fifth, we long more urgently for the unity of all Christians.

These fruits may appear to be a list of disconnected graces, or gifts, that one has received in the Sacrament of the Eucharist. But that is a misunderstanding. What the Eucharist offers as a sacrament is a foretaste of the heavenly banquet, of the perfect love in which each of us will participate in the beatific vision. In heaven, there is complete union with Christ. There is no sin, for the entire city of God is dedicated to the sacrifice of worship. The Church is not ripped apart by scandal or violence, but everyone sings in perfect harmony a sacrifice of praise to the Father. The saints, through the Eucharistic identity of heaven, have perfect love for the human family. They intercede for anyone who is hungry, thirsty, lonely, or longing for redemption in their lives.

At times, it may seem nearly impossible that a space of perfect love, of heavenly existence, could be experienced by us mortal human beings. Look around at the violence and poverty in cities, the scandal that often racks the Church, and the sins of men, women, and even systems that rip apart the social fabric.

But the Eucharist provides a pedagogy to form the maturing Christian to see more than can be immediately sensed. Here, it is wise to learn to see the world through the Eucharistic eyes of the Church's saints. At the end of her autobiography *The Long Loneliness*, the foundress of the Catholic Worker Movement (and Servant of God), Dorothy Day, writes about the Eucharistic vision needed to pierce through the sometimes mundane, sometimes even ugly aspects of existence:

> We cannot love God unless we love each other, and to love we must know each other. We know Him in the breaking of the bread, and we know each other in the breaking of bread, and we are not alone any more. Heaven is a banquet, and life is a banquet, too, even with a crust, where there is companionship. ... We have all known the long loneliness and we have learned that the only solution is love and that love comes with community.[13]

The pledge of future glory in the Eucharist is the total reception of divine love. The world is not yet a space that bows down in worship before such love. Sometimes, neither is the Church. And yet, that is why one approaches day after day, week after week, the Sacrifice of the Mass. Our future is Eucharistic, whether we recognize it or not.

The Catholic approaches the Eucharist, thus, as bread for the journey. Eucharistic worship is intended to slowly transfigure the world into a space of love. As Joseph Ratzinger concludes in *The Spirit of the Liturgy*, "Christian liturgy is liturgy on the way, a liturgy of pilgrimage toward the transfiguration of the world, which will only take place when God is 'all in all.'"[14] There is a union with God that is greater than can be experienced at any Mass. There is a communion in which we are called to partake within the Church that is not reducible to the petty power games that sometimes occupy parish life.

The Catholic lives in history, and the Eucharist is that unique sacrament that enables this complicated history to participate in Christ's sacrifice of love. Eucharistic worship takes time to bear fruit. And yet, when it begins to bear fruit in the life of the Church and the world alike, the most mundane aspects of the world are transformed. The Eucharistic Sacrifice transforms everything. At Mass, every aspect of my existence, through the prayer of the Church, is to be offered back to the Father. In his *Sacramentum Caritatis*, an apostolic exhortation on the Eucharist, Pope Benedict XVI writes:

> Christianity's new worship includes and transfigures every aspect of life: "Whether you eat or drink, or whatever you do, do all to the glory of God" (1 Cor 10:31). Christians, in all their actions, are called to offer true worship to God. Here the intrinsically eucharistic nature of Christian life begins to take shape. The Eucha-

rist, since it embraces the concrete, everyday existence of the believer, makes possible, day by day, the progressive transfiguration of all those called by grace to reflect the image of the Son of God (cf. Rom 8:29ff.). There is nothing authentically human — our thoughts and affections, our words and deeds — that does not find in the sacrament of the Eucharist the form it needs to be lived to the full. Here we can see the full human import of the radical newness brought by Christ in the Eucharist: the worship of God in our lives cannot be relegated to something private and individual, but tends by its nature to permeate every aspect of our existence. Worship pleasing to God thus becomes a new way of living our whole life, each particular moment of which is lifted up, since it is lived as part of a relationship with Christ and as an offering to God. The glory of God is the living man (cf. 1 Cor 10:31). And the life of man is the vision of God.[15]

In the Eucharistic worship of the Church, we are learning to live out our identities as creatures made for worship. We are not always perfect in this regard. But God has given us time to become what we receive in the Blessed Sacrament, a creature made for love unto the end.

This Eucharistic transformation points toward the redemption of all that is human. Marriage, as a sacrament, is a privileged way in which everything, including the mundaneness of the domestic Church, is transformed into a space of sacramental love. The next chapter thus extends our discussion of the Eucharist to the Sacrament of Marriage.

Chapter 4
Marriage as the Transformation of the Mundane

In the last chapter, we turned our attention to the Sacrament of the Eucharist. The Sacrament of the Eucharist is distinct from the other sacraments, because the *res et sacramentum* (the reality and sign together) of the Eucharist is the personal and sacramental presence of Jesus Christ. The Eucharist, while still manifesting the signs of bread and wine, becomes the Body and Blood of Christ through the priest or bishop speaking the words of Institution over the unleavened bread and the wine. Whereas, for example, baptismal water, consecrated to the Triune God, is not the substantial presence of Christ.

And yet, the Eucharist is not alone in standing out among

the sacraments. The Sacrament of Marriage has as its sign (*sacramentum tantum*) not a material object like bread and wine, but the exchange of consent between man and woman. In the Latin West, this act of consent is the moment of sacramental consecration whereby the husband and wife become a sign of Christ and the Church. Marriage, in all its mundaneness, reveals the evangelizing potential of all the sacraments. The day-to-day mission of loving one's spouse, raising children, and participating in social life may become an efficacious sign of divine love in the world.

The History of Marriage: Divine Love and Human Salvation

The historical development of the Sacrament of Marriage is itself a study of evangelization. Marriage as a natural institution is taken up and then sanctified through the Church. In the early Church, marriage would have been celebrated for the most part just as it was in Roman society in general. A wife was led out to the home of her husband, where there would have been an exchange of gifts, and then a formal incorporation of the wife into the husband's home. Early Christians recognized a healing and sanctifying dimension to Christian marriage, even if there was not an accompanying sacramental rite. Saint Augustine (writing against Saint Jerome's almost visceral abhorrence toward marriage, and thereby, creation) argues for three goods of marriage, including fidelity, the *sacramentum* or indissoluble bond, and procreation.[1] The *sacramentum* is indissoluble for Saint Augustine, because marriage is intended to reflect the original unity of God and the human race. The *sacramentum* of marriage — the nuptial bond between husband and wife that reflects the union of God with humanity — heals and sanctifies human sexuality. Marriage is a created good, and it is only made better through the Church.

After Augustine, more formal liturgical rites developed related to marriage. These rites often included blessings of the marriage bed, as well as a nuptial blessing over the wife thirty days after the formalized rite of marriage.[2] But, the rite of marriage in early medieval Catholicism was still primarily a domestic one, leading to potential problems. If it was a sacrament, what role did the Church play in the sacrament? A debate raged about what constituted — if marriage were a sacrament — the moment of consecration.[3] One theory suggested that it was the moment of consent. Consent was not equivalent to betrothal. To promise someone marriage (betrothal) was not the same thing as pledging lifelong fidelity (consent). If this fidelity was pledged (if this consent was given), using specific words, then the Sacrament of Marriage took place. A second theory argued that consummation was what consecrated marriage. Since marriage itself was so closely linked to procreation and sexual union, this made some sense. But there were significant difficulties with the theory of consummation. For example, consider the following. A couple is betrothed. During the betrothal, the man engages in intercourse with another woman. He later regrets this. He comes back, perhaps through the gentle persuasion of the law (in many cultures, a betrothal can have some level of enforcement), and seeks to return to the woman he originally intended to marry. But his lover says that he intended to marry her (although he had never explicitly consented to marry her), and that their act of intercourse was therefore a moment of consummation. Is he married? Is he not? Partially for occurrences such as these, canon lawyers and theologians agreed that consent was necessary for marriage, first, with consummation then "sealing" the indissoluble bond given in consent. Further, it was concluded that marriage must take place within a church building (or at least outside on the porch of the church), precisely because consent needed to be witnessed by an official minister of the Church.

Concurrent with developments in canon law related to marriage was a flowering of medieval monastic literature related to desire, love, and marriage.[4] St. Bernard of Clairvaux, admitting only mature men to his reformed Cistercian rule, recognized that many of these men had far more sexual experience than the child oblates in a typical Benedictine monastery. Rather than crush this desire through discipline, the monks were taught to redirect all desire to God. The kiss of the mouth, in the first verse of the Song of Songs, becomes "an unreserved infusion of joys, a revealing of mysteries, a marvelous and indistinguishable mingling of the divine light with the enlightened mind, which, joined in truth to God, is one spirit with him."[5] Celibate men and women began to interpret the consecrated life, often through exegesis of the Song of Songs, as a nuptial or spousal vocation.[6]

Through developments in both canon law and medieval exegesis of the Song of Songs, sacramental theologians began to acknowledge that marriage between a man and a woman was more than the restoration of a creation sacrament — the union of man and woman in Genesis. Hugh of Saint Victor, in his work *On the Sacraments*, describes marriage as a sign of the love between God and the soul, as well as Christ and the Church.[7] The act of consent was so important to Hugh of Saint Victor that sexual union might not have even been necessary for marriage, according to him. Marriage was a sacrament because it was an efficacious sign that both healed and sanctified in a natural and supernatural way.

In many accounts of the history of marriage, one often hears that marriage was not made a sacrament until the Council of Trent in the aftermath of the Reformation. This is an exaggeration. By the time of both Saint Bonaventure and St. Thomas Aquinas, marriage was understood as a sacrament whereby the couple comes, through the act of consent, to manifest the love of Christ and the Church in the nuptial union. Saint Bonaventure even upholds the gift of sexual union between husband and wife because this sexual union heals the original sin of concupiscence (disordered desire) introduced by the Fall.[8] In his *Summa Contra Gentiles*, St. Thomas Aquinas states that the couple receives the "gift" of Christ's love in marriage as part of the reception of the nuptial bond or the *res et sacramentum*. And through this reception, the couple "are included in the union of Christ and the Church, which is most especially necessary to them, that in this way in fleshly and earthly things they may purpose not to be disunited from Christ and the Church."[9] The natural quality of nuptial life, producing progeny and educating them, received grace through the grace of marriage.

In the years after the Council of Trent, there was an increasing awakening to the gift of marriage not only as a sanctified natural reality, but as a graced reality in the world that made available the love of Christ and the Church in human history. Earlier in this book, we encountered the writings of Matthias Joseph Scheeben. Even prior to Pope St. John Paul II, Scheeben was one of the first to express the sacramental transformation made possible through marriage. Marriage is not just one of the sacraments, but that sacrament which makes available to society the love of Christ and the Church in the union of husband and wife. The couple themselves become "sacraments." In his *Mysteries of Christianity*, he writes:

> It follows from the nature of Christian marriage that
> the husband and wife must love each other not merely
> with natural love, but with supernatural love, as mem-
> bers of Christ and as representatives of His mystical
> nuptials with the Church. They must love and honor,
> educate and rear, their children not only as the fruit of
> their own bodies, but as the fruit of the mystical nuptials
> mentioned, that is, as children of God. They must take

the place of Christ and the Church with regard to their
children, as their teachers, guardians, and models. This
is a lofty, supernatural vocation, which demands all the
greater graces. ... All these graces really come to them
from the marriage ... between Christ and the Church,
that marriage to which they are dedicated as organs, and
which is impressed, renewed, continued, and comple-
mented in their own union.[10]

Scheeben argues that marriage, although a natural reality, is ordered toward another end in the sacramental bond of Christian
marriage. The couple has a mission to become for their children
a sign of Christ and the Church. The deepening of this now supernatural union between husband and wife, a living sign of
Christ's love for the Church, is part of the grace, or gift, of love
given in the sacrament.

The writings of Pope St. John Paul II, particularly in his
Theology of the Body, further underline how divine love is made
available through the nuptial sacrament. In his commentary on
Ephesians 5:21–33, that most thorny of texts for preachers,[11]
John Paul II treats marriage not as the least of the sacraments,
but integral to the whole sacramental system. Sacramental marriages heal and sanctify men and women, allowing them to participate in the original vocation they were to assume before sin.
The submission of husband and wife is not first to each other,
but to Christ, who is the Bridegroom of the Church. John Paul
II states, "In the light of Ephesians — precisely through participation in the saving love of Christ — marriage as a sacrament
of the human 'beginning' is confirmed and at the same time renewed. It is the sacrament in which man and woman, called to
become 'one flesh,' participate in God's own creative love."[12] The
marriage bond is more than a contract. It is instead the bond of
love between Christ and the Church that transforms the mun-

daneness of married love into a graced reality in the world. Marriage and family life are sacraments of divine love, consecrating history into a space of divine love.

The Sacramental Rite of Marriage: A Personalistic Account of Sacramental Grace

One of the rites that received significant revision at the Second Vatican Council was *The Order of Celebrating Christian Matrimony*. The preconciliar Roman Ritual included the act of consent, but the Nuptial Blessing was reserved exclusively for the woman. After the Council, the Nuptial Blessing was recomposed to include the man as well, and was given immediately before the reception of the Eucharist.

This revision is essential to a deepening appreciation of the sacramentality of marriage. Like the Eucharist, marriage may be analyzed using the *sacramentum tantum, res et sacramentum*, and *res tantum*. And yet marriage, precisely because it is a sacrament that involves the exchange of consent of two persons, must be understood in a personalist mode.

Each chapter so far has already approached the sacraments in this personalist mode. The character, or seal, bestowed by certain sacraments is not just an objective mark upon the soul, but a union with the person of Jesus Christ, the God-man. The sacramental system cannot be reduced to the language of matter and form, but instead must always unfold in the context of an encounter with the living God.

Marriage is intrinsically such an encounter with God as mediated through the exchange of consent between the spouses. The *sacramentum tantum* of marriage is this exchange of consent. But what is consent?

Consent in marriage is not merely contractual language. In marriage, the consent is a free pledge of oneself to a man or a woman for as long as one lives. In the rite, consent commences with questions related to the freedom of the union, the willingness to recognize its indissoluble nature, and the openness to children. The couple then speaks their vows, given by the Church, pledging their lives to one another.

The specific words of the vows are given by the Church. Consent is an objective act. Couples may not write their own vows. This is not because the Church hates people who are in love. The formula that is given to the couple allows them to recognize the objective nature of the pledge. The vow itself is not constructed by the couple, because what is taking place is not a purely subjective expression of loving affection. It is not Meatloaf's "Paradise by the Dashboard Light," where love is pledged only because sexual desire is so powerful. A lifelong commitment is pledged objectively. A gift is bestowed.

When two baptized persons exchange this consent, there is a sacrament. Likely, you have heard before that the ministers of the Sacrament of Marriage are not the deacon, priest, or bishop, but the couple themselves. Too often this is presented as a conflict of power. At last, laypeople get to confect a sacrament. But power is not the reason why the couple serve as ministers of the sacrament. The couple are ministers because of what they are doing in the sacrament, at least within the Latin West. As baptized persons, they have both the right and responsibility to exercise their priesthood to consecrate the world unto God. In speaking this vow of lifelong fidelity, they are exercising this priesthood, uniting their act of mutual consent with God. In his commentary on the rite, the Catholic theologian of marriage and family, Cardinal Marc Ouellet, writes, "Through the act of mutual consent, the spouses in fact acquire a new participation in Christ's filiation in the Spirit, but now they participate as a couple, as the union of man and woman, in the communion of the Trinity, which is eternally one, fruitful, and indissoluble."[13] This speech act, this pledge of mutual fidelity, is a consecration of the act of consent. The couple is to manifest to the world the Trinitarian life of God, which is one, fruitful, and indissoluble. The Church is not accidentally present to this union, precisely because the couple has the capacity to offer this pledge through the Church in the first place. The presence of the minister, as well as the Nuptial Blessing, express the ecclesial nature of this sacrament.

This manifestation of Trinitarian love is not reducible to the verbal. Consummation of the nuptial union still matters. But again, consummation is not contractual. We cannot interpret consummation as "the deed is done, the sacrament is perfected." Rather, consummation is a sacramental sign whereby the act of consent becomes expressed through a flesh and blood encounter. The couple has pledged their lives to one another, expressed their openness to both union and life, and in sexual union they enact this self-gift. Sexual union in marriage is but a sign of the full meaning of consummation — the willingness to share a whole life together with one's spouse as a flesh and blood person. Turning once more to Cardinal Ouellet:

> The mutual "yes" expressed verbally in the liturgical celebration is then translated into the "language of the body," that is to say, not only into the conjugal encounter (consummation), but also into the spouses' shared life, daily fidelity, friendship, reciprocal forgiveness, fecundity, education, etc. The sacramental sign prolongs itself in time. The spiritual act of self-gift "in the Lord," enriched by the redemptive power of Christ and the salvific action of the Church, establishes the *couple* as a permanent sacrament and transforms its history into salvation history ... into a sign that bears the gift of God to his people.[14]

The *sacramentum tantum* extends itself in time. The act of consent, strictly speaking, involves the rest of the life of the couple, who instantiate consent every day. Sexual union and the whole life of the married couple, for the rest of their days, functions as an act of anamnesis, or sacramental remembering, of this self-giving love.[15] The couple makes present a love beyond all telling.

The couple becomes this sacramental sign, though not through their personal efforts. Sacramental marriage, like the rest of the sacraments, is not the result of moral excellence. The transformation in the couple's identity takes place through the *res et sacramentum*. Traditionally, in marriage, the *res et sacramentum* is understood as the nuptial bond that unites the couple together. Annulments, as we may know, testify that this nuptial bond was never there. Full consent was never bestowed.

A personalist perspective demands more, though, than treating the *res et sacramentum* as a contractual bond. If sacramental character is a relationship established with the God-man, Jesus Christ, so too is the nuptial bond, or the *res et sacramentum*. Indeed, early theologians debated whether marriage bestowed a character upon the couple. Because marriage could take place multiple times (in the case of the death of a spouse), and because it was so dependent on the freedom of consent, it was determined that marriage did not bestow a character. And yet, these same theologians noted that it bestowed something *like* a character upon the couple.

Ouellet describes the *res et sacramentum* as a charism bestowed upon the couple that transforms their identity. It is a gift — that is the meaning of charism — offered by God, consecrated through the Holy Spirit, that establishes a participation in the love of Christ and the Church at an objective level that transcends the subjective feelings of the couple.[16] It is for this reason that marriage is indissoluble. Catholics are not against divorce in the way that a politician may be for or against the passage of a law. Rather, Catholics state that if consent is given in perfect freedom, then there is an objective gift of God bestowed upon that couple that unites them as Christ and the Church. They are consecrated unto God. The bond only ends at death.

But, as Ouellet notes, participation in this bond is integral to the sacrament. Marriage is not magic, and it does not transform a poor union into a perfect one. As Ouellet writes, "The sanctification of the spouses, founded on baptism and marriage, will increase to the extent that they live out the charism that has made them 'one flesh,' a task requiring their openness to the particular graces that heal, purify, perfect, and even divinize their love."[17] Marriage is a change of the identity of the couple, but it is a transformation that necessitates a return-gift by the couple.

The couple is not left alone in offering this return-gift. The couple receives, through the Nuptial Union, the *res tantum* of both healing and sanctifying grace. Remember that grace is not an object. Grace is God's involvement in the life of the couple, here and now. The couple is not just exhorted to imitate the love of Christ and the Church. Rather, their marital love is a real participation in Christ's love for the Church through the day-to-day mission to love one another, do the dishes, take out the trash, bathe the children, go to work, teach, and pray together. The couple must undertake a spiritual journey to become increasingly open to the divine gift of love they have received in the sacrament. The gift that is Christ's love for the Church is present — although not substantially present — in the relationship of the couple.

The Sacrament of Marriage inserts the conjugal love of the couple into the love of Christ and the Church in such a way that even the goods of marriage mentioned by St. Augustine are transformed through a gift of grace. Marriage requires fidelity or "oneness" with husband or wife. There is a one-flesh union. Just as God was faithful to Israel, as Christ has been faithful to the Church, so too the couple are to be faithful to one another. The gift of love between husband and wife must be total. And for this reason, in marriage preparation, one must ascertain whether a total gift can be offered to one another. If a woman is an alcoholic who keeps her disease from her fiancé, or if a man is addicted to pornography and his fiancée is unaware, it is possible that fidelity or unity is not present from the beginning. Remember our principle: Sacraments effect by signifying, and since the couple's faithful love for one another is the sign, then that love must be faithful from the beginning. This does not mean perfect. After all, every person grows more fully into the art of self-giving love. But one must understand what this love involves, which includes possessing self-knowledge about one's own limitations.

Marriage is also, as we have seen, indissoluble. Such indissolubility is bestowed through the sacramental bond that is given in marriage. Since marriage is in Christ, it is a pledge of lifelong fidelity. As Ouellet comments on indissolubility, "Thanks to the marriage-sacrament, the bond between the spouses is completely removed from the arbitrary fluctuations of human sentiment. It is established as a sign and actualization of the nuptial bond by which Christ bound himself forever to his Church."[18] Once more, this is a difficult teaching. Many young people who approach the sacrament today have not been formed in an understanding of love, commitment, and the permanence of the nuptial bond — partially through their participation in a hookup culture, in which lifelong commitment, for the most part, is not in the equation.[19] In a hookup culture, love is reduced to an experience that one undergoes, and denying oneself potential experiences of happiness would be akin to self-torture.[20]

And yet, there may be occasions in which leaving one's spouse is the right decision. Domestic violence is real. Husbands and wives callously cheat on one another, often from the very beginning. As already hinted at, annulments are not Catholic divorces. They are investigations into what went wrong with the initial act of consent. The end of a spousal union is always hard. Annulments sometimes reveal that consent was never freely given in the first place. This does not mean that the marriage possessed no grace, or gift, of divine love. The sacraments bestow grace, but God does not give grace exclusively through the sacraments. At the same time, annulments are not always granted. I have talked to many spouses, whose husband or wife has left them. Sometimes they may wish they could get an annulment or divorce in order to get married again; yet, the spouse who has been abandoned often knows that the bond was authentically given. They therefore will not pursue another marriage. Even in this kind of sorrow, the grace of divine love is made present. Remember in the previous chapter what we said about Christ's hidden presence in the Eucharist. It is not perceptible to the senses. Similarly, even the hidden sacrifice of sorrow that an abandoned spouse endures can bear fruit. Those who are separated from their spouses and remain faithful to the sacramental bond, even if the other spouse does not, function as an efficacious sign of God's fidelity to the Church in the world. Even this sorrow becomes fruitful.

Ouellet also transforms fecundity into a good of marriage. You have likely heard people joke that Catholics are those with eight children, who purchase commercial vans to drive their brood around. While this may be a holdover from an earlier era, it nonetheless reveals a calculating logic to fertility that is not true to the personalist account of the Sacrament of Marriage we have taken up in this chapter. The first fruitfulness of marriage is not the guaranteed presence of children, but the fruitfulness of the triune God, of the sacrifice of Jesus Christ that unites the couple together. The couple is most fruitful when they open themselves to the fruitfulness of God. Even an infertile couple, who learn that they are unable to have children, participate in this fruitfulness. Their sorrow, the sacrifice of love they bestow on one another as they suffer, is part of the fruitfulness of marriage.

Fruitfulness is openness to life — this can look various ways. For example, a family might have eight kids, some adopted, some welcomed through foster care. This openness, knit into God's very love, is no longer purely a natural phenomenon. As Ouellet writes, "The child is not merely the result of their 'natural' love, but the fruit of their offering to God in faith, an offering that God blesses either with the gift of a child or with a gift of supernatural fruitfulness."[21] Fruitfulness is the couple's openness to another beyond each other; the love of the couple does not close in upon itself, but practices the radical hospitality of the Triune God. This is one of the reasons that contraception is not considered moral within the Catholic Church. Yes, families may need to make prudent decisions about how many children they may welcome into their home. Artificial contraception, though, often excludes this radical hospitality. It may lead to the couple treating their sexuality not as a gift open to life, but as a kind of exchange. After all, to receive the total gift of my spouse is to recognize that she is a human being who has the capacity to bear life. Our sexual union is not reducible to unadulterated pleasure, but must always be open to the possibility of another, in this case, the gift of a child. Catholic sex in marriage is about fruitful hospitality.

Whether a marriage results in the gift of a child or not, the union of husband and wife forms a domestic church. The term "domestic church" is not a metaphor — the family is like a church. The term "domestic church" denotes that in the Sacrament of Marriage, the "real presence" of sacramental communion is made manifest through the day-to-day life of the family. Ouellet concludes his discussion of marriage by saying:

The communion of life and love in the Christian family, founded on the "sincere gift of self" in the *sequela Christi*, goes beyond likeness to the trinitarian communion. It sacramentalizes the gift of the divine Persons to the world in Christ; it participates in, and grants access to, the exchange between the divine Persons in the Holy Spirit. Under the "species" of the spouses' fidelity, unity, and fecundity, a mystery of the covenant is accomplished, the covenant between the Trinity and the family, the domestic church. From this covenant are born sons and daughters of God, who bear witness that human love and divine love are capable not only of true reciprocity, but above all a *shared fruitfulness* in the grace of the Holy Spirit.[22]

The mundaneness of family life is not bereft of divine presence. Rather, it is within the context of this daily life of fidelity that divine love is made present.

Unfortunately, the language of the domestic church can easily be co-opted by an overly romantic account of familial life — perfect marriages that produce perfect children, who live perfect lives. These families do not exist.

It is for this reason that families require the entire sacramental life to sustain themselves. The Sacrament of the Eucharist serves as a prophetic sign of the family's deeper identity.[23] The family has been consecrated to God, sent on mission to transform their very lives into a Eucharistic offering for the sake of the world. The stability of the family is not given for the sake of the family alone, but so that the family may become a witness to the world of the divine love of the God-man, Jesus Christ.

One can see, thus, the evangelizing potential of the Sacrament of Marriage and the domestic church alike. The couple and the family must participate in this sacramental logic, learning the art of self-giving love. Through marriage and the family, we come to see how every dimension of reality may become, through the power of the Spirit, a sacramental sign of divine love in the world. As the theologian Cardinal Angelo Scola remarks, "Employing this sacramental dynamic in the life of the couple all the way to the end, it is no longer possible to be scandalized ... by the triviality and apparent banality of everyday life or by the weakness of the bridegroom and the bride."[24] In the family, even in the weakness of spouses and children alike, divine love takes flesh through the sacraments of the Church.

What marvelous news! God can sanctify everything, even sin and sickness, as we will see in the next chapter.

Chapter 5
Sin and Death: Consecrating Our Diminishments

Thus far, we have attended to the sacraments as efficacious signs which allow us to grow into perfect union with Jesus Christ. Through baptism, we are regenerated by the Holy Spirit into sons and daughters of God. Confirmation is a maturation of our baptismal character, sending us out on mission to offer spiritual sacrifices in praise of God. In the Eucharist, we offer a perfect Sacrifice, and at the same time we receive this love through eating and drinking Christ's Body and Blood. Holy Orders consecrates men to act in the person of Christ and the Church so that the Eucharistic Sacrifice might be available for the priesthood of the baptized. In matrimony, the love of Christ and the Church, available in each sacrament, becomes incarnate in the life of a couple, who sanctify the world through their nuptial union.

Still, we know that human life does not consist exclusively of growth. The athlete who once was the fastest man in the world may one day be no quicker than the average twenty-year-old. The brilliant student of physics may give up study because she is undisciplined. A beloved spouse may succumb to cancer. The Jesuit Catholic priest Teilhard de Chardin writes about these diminishments of human life:

> The internal passivities of diminishment form the darkest element and the most despairingly useless years of our life. Some were waiting to pounce on us as we first awoke: natural failings, physical defects, intellectual or moral weaknesses. … Others were lying in wait for us later on and appeared as suddenly and brutally as an accident, or as stealthily as an illness. All of us one day or another will come to realize, if we have not already done so, that one or other of these sources of disintegration has lodged itself in the heart of our lives. … And if by chance we escape … there still remains that slow, essential deterioration which we cannot escape: old age little by little robbing us of ourselves and pushing us towards the end. Time, which postpones possession, time which tears us away from enjoyment, time which condemns us all to death — what a formidable passivity is the passage of time.[1]

God does not leave us bereft in these passivities of diminishment. If the God-man, Jesus Christ, took up every dimension of the human condition, he also sacramentally transformed human diminishment through the Paschal Mystery. Through the Sacraments of Penance and the Anointing of the Sick, the Church encounters the crucified and risen Lord, who both heals and sanctifies. Reflecting on these sacraments together, we learn that evangelization does not consist merely of extraordinarily happy youth ministers who run social icebreakers. Evangelization is the sacramental transformation of every dimension of human life — even sin and death.

Sin and Death in Salvation History

I suspect few of us are comfortable with the relationship between sin and death expressed in the Scriptures. Sin, to us, is a conscious decision to reject God. On the other hand, death is something that even the holiest person undergoes. Is this not why we cry out in sorrow in situations when a very good person, holy in every way, is diagnosed with a terminal illness? Do we not ask ourselves, "Why him?" or "Why her?"

The Scriptures connect sin and death with one another, whether we are comfortable with it or not. Our task is to understand why. Genesis 3 presents to us the very first sin of humankind. God has given both Adam and Eve a paradise of delight, creating everything as a sign of love for those creatures he has made in his image and likeness. The only law in Paradise is that Adam and Eve may not eat of the tree of the knowledge of good and evil, lest they die. And yet, Eve is tempted by the serpent to do just that. The temptation is well-chosen by the crafty serpent. The serpent tells Eve that perhaps God has denied this food to them because God is stingy, refusing to allow them to share in divine life. Eve agrees, wanting to become like God through force. Adam is no better, and perhaps even worse. He eats the fruit from Eve without question, doubting the possibility that the good God, who created everything out of love, might possibly forgive.

In the case of both Adam and Eve, there is a denial of one's identity as creature, totally dependent upon God for all that is good. Joseph Ratzinger, in his commentary on Genesis 3, writes:

> We can at once say that at the very heart of sin lies human beings' denial of their creatureliness, inasmuch as they refuse to accept the standard and the limitations that are implicit in it. They do not want to be creatures, do not want to be subject to a standard, do not want to be dependent. They consider their dependence on God's creative love to be an imposition from without. ... Thus human beings want to be God. When they try this, everything is thrown topsy-turvy.[2]

The effect of this sin, of denying one's status as creature, is immediate violence introduced into the divine communion between Adam, Eve, and the created order. They realize they are naked, choosing uncomfortable fig leaves for their clothing. They no longer know how to relate to creation aright. God asks Adam if they have eaten of the tree, and Adam's response is a perfect expression of the rebelliousness of the hardened sinner: "The man said, 'The woman whom you gave to be with me, she gave me fruit of the tree, and I ate'" (Gn 3:12). Adam does not accept responsibility for his transgression, but blames God and Eve alike. Adam and Eve, at the end of this tragic dialogue, are placed outside of Paradise. The Tree of Life, with which God was to feed them, is no longer to be theirs. They will die, apart from Eden. In trying to seize divine life, they have lost it.

Likely, you know that Genesis is not a journalistic account of what took place when human beings first sinned. Rather, it is a theological account, concerned with the meaning of creation and sin. A good Jewish reader of the Fall narrative would recognize their own story in the drama of Adam and Eve. God had bestowed upon the twelve tribes of Israel the Promised Land as a gift. And yet, through worshiping other gods, and entering into covenants with other nations, Israel had transgressed against God. Rather than repent, they doubled down. And for this reason, the kingdom of Judah was conquered by Babylon, the Temple destroyed, and the Promised Land was lost. To be outside of God's good favor, to be under such judgment, was death for Israel. As the biblical theologian Gary Anderson writes, "In the … language of Israel's covenant charter, death was not defined simply as the termination of life. Death meant being deprived of God's blessing and bereft of life within his holy land."[3] Human beings, who no longer abide within the Promised Land, suffer from the absence of divine blessing.

Death, therefore, in the Scriptures, is not just the end of physical life. It is the experience of being cut off from communion with both God and one's neighbor. By making ourselves into God, seizing an identity that can only be received as gift, we die.

We Christians know that death is not the final answer. Jesus Christ comes in the Gospels to offer a liberating salvation for all. Is this not why Jesus Christ so often heals in the Gospels? And when he heals, notice how often Jesus also forgives sins.

In the Gospel of Luke, it is often impossible to separate the two occurrences. In Luke 5, Jesus heals a paralyzed man who is lowered through the roof. His friends were the ones who lifted this man up, taking him up to the roof, and lowering him down. Jesus, upon witnessing this act of communion, the refusal to let the sick man be alone, forgives the sins of the sick man. He does so after seeing the faith of his friends who remain in communion with the person who is sick. The Pharisees object. Who gave Jesus the power to forgive sins? Jesus challenges the Pharisees, noting that the Son of Man has authority both to forgive sins and to heal. The two are linked.

In his commentary on the Gospel of Luke, the biblical theo-

logian Paul S. Minear highlights why Jesus links these two dimensions of his ministry. Jesus Christ is the final and greatest
prophet, coming at the end of time, to announce the end of the
reign of sin and death. Minear writes:

> To the evangelist the invasion of the powers of the king-
> dom marked the greater change, with the healing of the
> sick a secondary sign of that change. It was the gospel
> preached to the poor that effected their liberation; it was
> by faith in that gospel that men were cured of all man-
> ner of impotence and hopelessness, with repercussions
> in manifold kinds of psychic and somatic release.[4]

Through Jesus Christ, God has come to enter fully into communion with the human family. Sickness is a sign that the endless
diminishments of human life, an existence seemingly devoid of
divine blessing, are coming to an end.

These miracle accounts are not the only healing in which Jesus engages. The self-emptying love of Jesus, leading to his death
on the cross, is the privileged healing that he offers to the human
family.[5] Jesus is the one who is totally innocent. And still, Jesus
dies upon the cross and descends into the realm of the dead.
This realm, called Sheol, was the place where there was no communion with God or neighbor. One was cut off. But, as Ratzinger writes, "In Christ, God himself entered that realm of death,
transforming the space of noncommunication into the place of
his own presence. This is no apotheosis of death. Rather has God
canceled out and overcome death in entering it through Christ."[6]
The word *apotheosis* means the "highest point" or "development."
We focus, as Christians, on the death of Christ, not because we
are masochists. Rather, the death of Jesus is God's entrance into
the place of noncommunion. God descends into the darkness of
human sin and death with willing, total, self-giving love.

Remember that it was our first parents, Adam and Eve, who introduced sin and death into the world. They did so by seizing control, trying to become like gods through force. They wanted to make themselves immortal. Christ does not follow that path of Adam and Eve. He is the one who, in Paul's letter to the Philippians, is described as refusing to seize or grasp identity with God. He instead empties himself in the totality of love unto the end. His sacrifice of love is accepted by the Father, and he is raised from the dead.

And in all this, Jesus takes up our sin and death with him, offering it upon the cross. "Atonement" is the word that the Church uses to refer to the reconciliation, or healing, that Jesus' death effected. This death did not placate an angry Father-God, who needed to see human flesh and blood suffer. Rather, this free death of Jesus Christ was God's dazzling act of love for men and women. He loved us unto the end, despite our hardened hearts. Communion with God is now possible even in the darkest hours of our lives, where we feel most separated from God.

The theologian Hans Urs von Balthasar notes that we as Christians still experience this healing through Christ. He writes:

> If we are afraid of dying because we do not know how to do this: to consent to being swept away as a whole, then we should not forget that someone was able to do it for us beforehand, someone who did not die as some individual next to us, but who, dying and suffering, already bore our death in himself. ... In death he has accomplished this complete surrender within our fear, our inability, our insurmountable unwillingness, and this not for himself, but for our sake, so that in this same act he has transferred all of his achievement eucharistically into us.[7]

In taking on the human condition, including all its darkness, Jesus manifests to us that we too can discover a renewal of communion in this darkness. God does not abandon us here. And in an analogous way to the Eucharist, the signs of this darkness — including sin and death — may become the very place where God was dwelling with us all along.

Confession as a Sacrifice of Love

The history of penance as a sacrament is, like marriage, somewhat complicated. In the biblical period, there was no ritual way of confessing one's sins. Forgiveness of sin took place throughout the course of normal Christian life.

But soon, Christians committed sins that seemed to require more than regular participation in the Eucharistic Liturgy. An Order of Penitents was established for those Christians who committed serious sin such as apostasy, murder, or adultery after baptism. In describing this order, the liturgical historian Antonio Santantoni writes, "In the daily life of the penitent, everything was mortification and renunciation. There were strict fasts repeated numerous times during the week, a pallet strewn with ashes for a bed, prolonged vigils, hundreds of genuflections and prostrations repeated morning and night, abstinence from meat, and the obligation to give alms."[8] Formal reconciliation of the penitent would take place on either Holy Thursday in Rome or Milan, or Good Friday in Spain. The origins of Ash Wednesday (including the sprinkling of ashes upon the forehead) may be found in this Order of Penitents. And often, it was the feet of those in the Order of Penitents which were washed, reintegrating them into the community.

As one might imagine, based on its severity, the Order of Penitents declined in late antiquity. But confession of sin did not disappear. Celtic monasticism developed manuals of penance for monks to use. These manuals were also applied in various pastoral situations. Baptized Christians who were not monks also participated in regimes of penance. Over the next centuries, the regime of public penance and confession would combine into a single rite. This tenth-century rite included a penitent approaching a confessor, as well as undergoing an examination related to the central mysteries of the Faith. The penitent was admonished to forgive all those who committed sins against himself, asked a series of questions related to his sins, given a penance, allowed to express his sins in his own words, and directed to lie prostrate on the floor while saying Psalm 22.[9]

This practice of confessing one's sins became increasingly popular through the preaching of the reformed religious orders (the Franciscans and Dominicans) in the twelfth and thirteenth centuries. In 1215, the Fourth Lateran Council declared that one must receive the Eucharist once per year, going to confession before receiving the Blessed Sacrament at Easter. Concurrently, the matter of the sacrament was defined as the acts of the penitent (including the confession of sins), while the form was the priest speaking the words, "I absolve you ... "[10]

At the Second Vatican Council, there was a significant reform of the Order of Penance. Rather than a single rite, there became three options for the rite of penance. There is a rite for reconciliation of an individual penitent, a rite for several penitents with individual confession, and a rite for reconciliation of penitents with general confession and absolution. This last rite is reserved for those times in which a penitent may not individually confess sins (such as cases of immediate fear of death).

Importantly, each rite presumes that the sacrament takes place as an act of worship, rather than a private confession to a priest on a Saturday afternoon. Even when one is celebrating the rite with an individual penitent, it is assumed that there is a reading of the Word of God, confession of sin and acceptance of penance, and a prayer offered by the penitent along with the words of the priest, "I absolve you from your sins in the name of the Father and of the Son and of the Holy Spirit."

Yet, it is well known that participation in the Sacrament of Penance, Confession, or Reconciliation — depending on one's preferred nomenclature — has declined. While there may be a variety of reasons for this, including increasing distrust in the institution of the Church and the lack of public opportunities to celebrate the sacrament (Saturday afternoon from 4:00–4:07 p.m. is not normally the best time for families), one major reason for its decline is a modern dislike of the language of sin.

A sacramental theology of penance requires attention to sin. Likely, you remember the major two categories of sin in Catholicism. There are mortal sins that cut us off from communion with God and our neighbor, and there are venial sins that are daily transgressions that are forgiven through fasting, prayer, and almsgiving. If I murder my neighbor, watch pornography by choice each day, or cheat on my spouse, I have committed mortal sins. If I mumble rudely under my breath, or yell at my child for no reason, I have likely committed a venial sin. Mortal sins require one to go to confession before receiving the Eucharist. Venial sins do not. These latter sins are forgiven through a daily life of prayer and penance.

And yet, we must be careful lest these categories become treated in a legal rather than a personal manner. Sin cannot be reduced to breaking various laws, which necessitate participation in a sacrament. Sin is my warped desire to turn myself into God. Sin is when I reorder the world according to my image and likeness, rather than the received wisdom of God. It is a denial of my status as creature, as one who is made to worship God rather than myself.

Because sin is always a form of self-worship, the medicine of the sacrament is turning back to worship God. The Sacrament of Penance or Reconciliation is called by a variety of names. It is a sacrament of conversion, in which I hear Jesus' call to conversion in my life. It is a sacrament of penance "since it consecrates the Christian sinner's personal and ecclesial steps of conversion, penance, and satisfaction."[11] Notice the language of consecration. The word *consecration* is used to describe the transformation of the Eucharist into the Body and Blood of Christ. This sacrament is likewise called confession since I admit before the priest my sins. The sacrament is similarly one of forgiveness and reconciliation, since I personally receive sacramental absolution of my sins, while also being reconciled to full communion with the Church.

In this sacrament, there is a conversion that takes place. The liturgy for each of the three possible rites presumes that we first hear the Word of God in the Sacred Scriptures, calling us to return. This return is not exclusively out of a sense of fear, but rather love. I see the gift of love that is offered in Jesus Christ's life, death, and resurrection. There is a totality to the gift, which is not reflected in my life. I was created in the image and likeness of God, re-created through the Sacrament of Baptism, consecrated through confirmation, and invited every day to receive the Body and Blood of Christ. And yet, I too often find myself apathetic about these gifts I have received from God. As Matthias Scheeben writes about sin, "Sin not only opposes the law of God, not only resists God as Lawgiver, not only besmirches the dignity and position of the sinner; it runs counter to his own interior hunger and love of God and God's law, counter to his own interior justice and goodness."[12] Conversion is the recognition that one is made for more.

In this sense, sacramental penance necessitates that I live a penitential life outside of the celebration of the sacrament alone. Remember that the matter of the Sacrament of Penance is the conversion of the penitent him- or herself. The *Catechism* states,

"Reading Sacred Scripture, praying the Liturgy of the Hours and the Our Father — every sincere act of worship or devotion revives the spirit of conversion and repentance within us and contributes to the forgiveness of our sins."[13] Conversion, in the sacrament, is not undertaken ten minutes before the penitent goes to confession. It is a form of life, in which I learn to offer the return-gift of my love back to the God who first loved me.[14]

This life of conversion, of contrition for our sins, must also be verbally confessed. This is often where many struggle with the Sacrament of Penance, or Reconciliation. Why must I confess my sins aloud to a priest? Remember that the priest is not acting in his own person. He is acting in the person of Jesus Christ and the Church. Only God forgives sins, and the priest is acting as an instrument for God to work through the sacrament.

There is more to this confession of sins than the priest becoming an instrument of God's forgiveness. When I speak aloud my sins, I am in fact engaging in an act of worship. How so? To confess my sins aloud to a priest is not an act of therapy. Rather, I am acknowledging to God that I am a creature rather than the Creator. I am not God. I am annoyed, sometimes, with my children. I am not sufficiently reverent before the Eucharistic Mystery at Mass. I consciously and often lazily choose not to love unto the end. In speaking the sins aloud, I am acknowledging that they are mine. I am not blaming another person for the sins I have committed. They are all mine, and now I give them back to God with a contrite heart. I am a creature, in need of the gift of love, rather than the false narrative of self-sufficiency.

In offering this confession, though, I am not left alone. Quite literally, I am confessing to another person who is acting not only in the person of Christ, but of the entire Church. This is important! At Mass, we pray the *Confiteor*. In this prayer, we ask God for forgiveness for all the sins that we have committed, either intentionally or through omission. And we acknowledge that these sins are entirely our fault — "through my fault, through my fault, through my most grievous fault." In confessing my sins and thus acknowledging myself as creature, I now recognize that other creatures exist too. There are others who are in relationship with me, assisting me in my pursuit of divine life. They include angels, the saints, and our fellow creatures at worship with us. There is a creaturely solidarity in confessing our sins. We are not God, but happily we are not God together.

Still, my refusal to love God and neighbor has had negative consequences. Because of my sin, I owe something back to God and neighbor alike. I possess a debt. The *Catechism* describes this debt as follows:

> Many sins wrong our neighbor. One must do what is possible in order to repair the harm (e.g., return stolen goods, restore the reputation of someone slandered, pay compensation for injuries). Simple justice requires as much. But sin also injures and weakens the sinner himself, as well as his relationships with God and neighbor. Absolution takes away sin, but it does not remedy all the disorders sin has caused. Raised up from sin, the sinner must still recover his full spiritual health by doing something more to make amends for the sin: he must "make satisfaction for" or "expiate" his sins. This satisfaction is also called "penance."[15]

Now, it may be hard to believe that the penance with which we are normally bestowed when we go to the sacrament is linked to repairing any harm that we have done. How does praying three Our Fathers and three Hail Marys fix the fact that I yelled at my kids?

In one sense, it is an act of restoration insofar as I receive the penance from the priest and take it up without fighting against it. I am receiving my medicine, which in the case of sin is an act of obedient love. And I am not forced to pray that Our Father or Hail Mary at record pace. I could follow the path of St. Teresa of Ávila in her way of perfection where she describes how to use mental prayer in praying the Our Father. The purpose of this prayer is not to move as quickly as possible to show God that we know the words. Rather, in the first words of the prayer, we can spend time like Teresa acclaiming, "O my Lord, how you do show yourself to be the Son of such a Father! May you be blessed forever and ever!"[16]

In another sense, the typical penances bestowed do not conform themselves to the purpose of the sacrament. The penance should respond to the personal needs of the penitent. If that penitent is afraid of feeding the poor, she should be given a penance to do just that. If a father is impatient with his daughter, he should be given a penance to cultivate the virtue of patience.

These penances, whatever they are, are not a way in which we lift ourselves up by our bootstraps, ascending back to God. After all, it is always Christ who is acting in the life of the baptized, bringing us to conversion, enabling us to offer the spiritual sacrifice of our lives. And while the *sacramentum tantum* of sacramental penance is the conversion of the sinner, the *res et sacramentum* is Christ's own restoration of the bond of love between the individual and the Church. As Scheeben describes, the whole work of conversion, penance, and satisfaction is Christ's own work:

> The cancellation of the debt, as also the return of grace, is rooted in the character of the member of Christ, on the strength of which that member can do satisfaction himself and participate in the satisfaction of Christ, as well as share in Christ's merits and the power of His grace.[17]

This whole journey of conversion and confession is consecrated to God through the act of penance. The sacrament is not a program of self-improvement. Rather, through the Sacrament of Penance, the Church prays for God to consecrate and thus transform my sinfulness into an opportunity for Christ to act in my life. Through the sacrament, Jesus seeks to restore friendship with the Christian. The end of penance is greater participation in Christ's life and thus the life of the Church. Absolution forgives my personal sins, but it also reconciles me to the Church. My restoration is good news for the whole communion of believers, who welcome me back to the Eucharistic altar. From the beginning, the Sacrament of Penance has been ordered toward the worship of God.

Anointing of the Sick as a Sacrifice of Love

Sickness is a physical ailment that is also spiritual. Think about the COVID-19 pandemic. The pain of someone suffering from COVID-19 is not reducible to the symptoms that one is experiencing. Rather, it includes being cut off from the communion that human beings are called to enjoy with one another. The quarantined patient with COVID-19 is not only coughing with a fever, but feels entirely alone, a kind of leper whom no one wants to be close to.

Terminal illness is especially lonely, even if it is not attached to this same kind of judgment. Anyone who has been in a hospital and heard the words, "It's cancer," knows what I am saying. At this moment, the cancer patient feels alone. She has been diagnosed with a contagion that seemingly no one else around her possesses. Relationships that she imagined might last for decades are now in question. And with a terminal diagnosis, this patient is likely to ask herself, "Where is God?"

We may experience, in such illness, sheer passivity before the tremendous possibility of death. But the Christian does not live existence in this way. Everything has been transformed through the power of Christ, including illness. As the introduction to the rites found in the *Pastoral Care of the Sick* states:

> Suffering and illness have always been among the greatest problems that trouble the human spirit. Christians feel and experience pain as do all other people; yet their faith helps them to grasp more deeply the mystery of suffering and to bear their pain with greater courage. From Christ's words they know that sickness has meaning and value for their own salvation and for the salvation of the world. They also know that Christ, who during his life often visited and healed the sick, loves them in their illness.[18]

The Sacrament of the Anointing of the Sick is a consecration of sickness for the benefit of the sick person and the entire Church. Through this anointing, the sick person gives their whole self over to God as a sacrifice of love.

This may be a surprising way to look at the anointing of the sick. Many people who know anything about this sacrament think about it exclusively as a rite for the dying. Immediately before death, a Christian is to be anointed with oil, forgiven of his or her sins, and receive Viaticum — or their last Eucharistic communion — if they can. Most Catholics still presume that this sacrament is what the Church once called Extreme Unction, an anointing when one is in danger of death.

Up until the eighth century, this sacrament of anointing was given to any person who was ill. It was even likely administered not by a bishop or a priest, but a family member.[19] But by the time of St. Thomas Aquinas, the sacrament had been reserved exclusively for those who were dying, and administered by clergy. He writes in his *Summa Contra Gentiles*, "Hence, it is clear that this sacrament is the last, that it somehow tends to consummate the entire spiritual healing, and that in it a man is, as it were, prepared for the perception of glory."[20] In the midst of sickness, sins are forgiven, and a particular gift of divine love is offered by Christ who assists the baptized Christian to attain his or her final end.[21]

The reformed rites of the Second Vatican Council, while recognizing that many receive this sacrament before death, teach that the anointing of the sick is not reserved exclusively for those who are dying. Rather, it may be bestowed upon anyone who is suffering from serious illness or old age. The sacrament includes the signs of laying on of hands, praying over the ill, anointing the sick with blessed oil, and if possible, receiving the Eucharist. The anointing with oil is the *sacramentum tantum* and the matter of the sacrament, while the prayer offered by the presbyter over the sick during the anointing is the sacramental form.

The prayer after anointing reveals what has taken place through the laying on of hands and the anointing with oil. In the case of an extreme or terminal illness, the priest prays:

Lord Jesus Christ,
you chose to share our human nature,
to redeem all people, and to heal the sick.

Look with compassion upon your servant N.,
whom we have anointed in your name with this
holy oil
for the healing of his/her body and spirit.

Support him/her with your power,
comfort him/her with your protection,
and give him/her the strength to fight against evil.

> Since you have given him/her a share in your own
>   passion,
>   help him/her to find hope in suffering,
>   for you are Lord for ever and ever.[22]

Notice what this prayer states. Jesus Christ is the God-man, who shares fully in the human condition. He became flesh for the healing of all humanity. And yet, right now, it is this concrete person who is sick, this servant of God. The anointing is bestowed for the sake of the healing of both the body and the spirit. But the prayer does not declare that the sick person will be healed. Rather, it asks that God will support, comfort, and bestow strength upon the sick person. The sickness itself is a sharing in the passion of Christ, one that enables the sick person to find hope and meaning in suffering.

The sick person has been consecrated to Christ, and now that person dwells in relationship with Jesus. He or she is not alone. Christ is there, mediated through the oil and the laying on of hands. Further, the rite is to be celebrated, ideally, not alone, but in the presence of the faithful or at least the family. The precarious loneliness of sickness is transformed through the presence of Christ in the sacramental rites.

The hand-laying, in fact, reveals the meaning of the entire sacrament.[23] No matter how we feel, our communion with God and one another as baptized Catholics cannot be severed. While experiencing acute loneliness, the hand of the minister reaches out to touch the sick body. The healing that is enacted in those moments need not be an immediate cure of cancer, but it is the soothing touch of Christ and the Church bestowing comfort in the life of this sick person.

The anointing of the sick, if possible, is celebrated in the context of the Eucharist — whether at Mass or with the reception of Holy Communion. Having been anointed, the sick person participates in the Eucharist. Once more, we return to the spiritual sacrifice that the sick person is to offer. It is not just that this sickness is to have meaning for him or her. Instead, this act of suffering in union with Christ is a gift that is offered for the whole Church.

For many, this act of Eucharistic reception is Viaticum, the last time that the baptized Christian will receive the Body and Blood of Christ in the Eucharist. This moment of Eucharistic reception is part of what transforms death into a sweet rest in Christ. The sacramental theologian Fr. James T. O'Connor writes about Viaticum:

> That same Lord present in the Eucharist is our companion on the way to that rest where, journey done, we shall see him face to face. It is the gift we desire for all the dead: "Eternal rest grant unto them, O Lord." It is not the rest of sleep. It is the rest of God, the rest of the Lord, the rest promised to those who do not harden their hearts, who do not have hearts of stone but hearts of flesh, since it is the heart of flesh that is required in that rest whose activity is love.[24]

The person dying, we dare to hope through the merits of Jesus Christ, is going to see God face-to-face. No longer in need of the sacraments, no longer in need of any mediation, their very existence will be an act of praise to God. Through the offering of their illness, through the reception of the Blessed Sacrament, their very self will become a perfect offering of praise.

Thus, the evangelizing potential of the sacraments is not only for those who experience no diminishment. Every dimension of human life, through the sacraments, may be offered back to God. The task of the Church is to form men and women in the proper dispositions to celebrate this sacramental life. This sacramental formation — and its pastoral consequences — is the theme of the final chapter of this book.

Chapter 6
Cultivating Dispositions for a Sacramental Life

In chapter one of this book, we began by asking a question: What are sacraments, and why do they matter? Over the course of five chapters, we discovered that sacraments are the way that God both heals and sanctifies men and women through efficacious signs. Sacraments consecrate us, in Christ, so that we may offer our lives as a spiritual sacrifice through Christ to the Father by the power of the Holy Spirit.

This book has proposed the evangelizing quality of the sacraments of Catholicism. And yet, we know that the divine offer of love — that is, the gift of grace — bears fruit in those who receive the sacraments with the proper dispositions. Cultivating these dispositions is the privileged task of sacramental formation.

This final chapter, therefore, serves both as a summary of what we have learned thus far, and a pastoral exploration of the evangelizing end of sacramental formation. Dispositions, or capacities, must be cultivated through a sacramental catechesis that offers the richest possible account of the sacramental life: the creation of a world oriented toward love.

Sacraments Evangelize by Efficaciously Signifying

Remember in the first chapter that we dealt with a popular phrase in pastoral circles. A cultural Catholic is likely sacramentalized, but not evangelized. We recognized that the phrase, although expressing something true about disaffiliation, did not sufficiently recognize that it is Christ who is acting in the sacraments. We proposed instead that someone may have received the sacraments, but not yet produced fruit.

Part of the problem with acknowledging the sacraments as intrinsically evangelizing is an attenuated, or thin, account of both evangelization and the sacraments. Evangelization is often treated as the religious response of the individual to the kerygma, or proclamation, of the Gospel. The evangelized are those who have experienced a personal relationship with Jesus Christ, and for this reason long to participate in the Church through initiation, the sacramental life, and continuing catechesis. There is an intentionality that is required for evangelization. And the evangelizing task tends to be directed to the individual, who must be converted to authentically participate in Christ's life through the Church.

The problem with this account of evangelization is that it treats evangelization more as a task directed exclusively to a person, and less as the very mission of the Church. Evangelization becomes inviting someone to a Bible study, then leading them to more frequent participation in Mass, and then to a total commitment to ecclesial life. All of this is good; it is indeed evangelizing for the person and the whole Church. But this act of evangelization does not encompass all that the Church means by the phrase. The *Directory for Catechesis* says:

> Evangelizing is … making present and announcing Jesus Christ. The Church's mission of evangelization best expresses the economy of Revelation; in fact the Son of God is made flesh, enters into history; and becomes human among humanity. Evangelization makes this enduring presence of Christ concrete, in such a way that those who draw near to the Church may encounter in his person the way to "save their lives" (cf. Mt. 16:25) and open themselves to a new horizon.[1]

Evangelization is the concrete manifestation of the presence of Jesus Christ in the world. Jesus has not left humankind orphans. And in the case of the sacramental life, each of the sacraments manifests the God-man's activity *here and now*. The baptized infant (even in a culturally Catholic, albeit non-practicing, family) is truly united to Jesus Christ through the reception of the sacramental character. He or she is a son or daughter of God, who is mystically in union with the person of Jesus Christ through the power of the Spirit. This relationship is not first dependent on the infant's response. God always makes the first move.

Every baptism or confirmation, each celebration of the Mass, and every marriage liturgy is an act of evangelization by the Church. Humankind and the world are consecrated unto the triune God. And yet, we often forget this, not only because our account of evangelization is too thin, but because we also do not possess a rich enough explanation of the sacraments themselves. Sacraments too often are only considered "to work" when the one who is receiving the sacrament is sincerely aware of what is taking place. Sacramental sincerity is the necessary qualification, at least according to many Catholics, for receiving the sacraments.

The language of sincerity is characteristic of modern ritual life. While our Catholic forebears presumed that the rites of the Church did something unto themselves, we expect that one must engage in these rites exclusively in an authentic manner if they are to be truly meaningful. Individuals must "experience" meaningful rites, lest they act inauthentically. In a recent work, this kind of liturgical or ritual sincerity is described as relying "on internally generated knowledge and motivation."[2] The effectiveness of prayer, and its capacity to assist me in expressing myself, are dependent on whether or not I both understand what is happening in the prayer, and that I feel like I want to pray. I must choose it.

I often hear something like this when I speak to my undergraduate students on prayer. They are regularly dismissive of ritual or rote prayer, insofar as it is not an authentic expression of their affections. Sure, their parents taught them the Our Father, ensured that they received first Communion, and pushed them to receive the Sacrament of Confirmation. But it was not until they truly "felt" God — for example, on a retreat in their junior year of high school — that they "made faith their own." They look back at what they did earlier as going through the motions, often without a lot of meaning.

This assumption is not reserved for my undergraduates. I often hear Catholics say that they wish everyone could go through an RCIA or OCIA program so that every Catholic would really know what they believe. A richer understanding of the Catholic Faith is an admirable end of all catechesis. But the assumption behind this claim is that the Catholic who has not experienced RCIA is only going through the motions. They participate in the "signs" of the sacraments without understanding what the sacraments mean.

Applying this idea to the sacraments, the Church today has perhaps overemphasized the "sign" aspect of the sacraments, without attending to the status of the sacraments as "efficacious." The "sign" aspect of the sacraments, of course, can never be left behind. Our principle remains: The sacraments effect by signifying. Still, the sacraments are not just about my meaningful participation in Christ's life. Rather, they relate to what God is doing objectively in the world through the action of the Church. The person who goes to Mass each Sunday, without total awareness of what is happening in the Eucharistic prayer, is still participating in God's objective, transformative activity.

And we must keep in mind that what God is objectively giving in the sacraments is the very life of God, bestowed through sacramental signs. The sacraments are occasions of God's revelation to us as creatures. They are the presence of the triune God, acting in the world through the ministry of the Church. When Mass is celebrated, even among three people in a chapel in a city, Jesus Christ comes to reveal himself.

Does this mean that we are left with nothing more than a kind of "magical" account of the sacraments? The sacraments do what they do, and our response does not matter? Of course not! The sacraments are efficacious as signs, which communicate to us. But how do signs communicate in the first place?

For the theologian Hans Urs von Balthasar, God's communication in Divine Revelation happens in an aesthetic mode. Aesthetics, as a term, relates to art, beauty, and every act of perception in which a human being engages. Since human beings are embodied, material creatures, then God must communicate to us in an aesthetic, or perceptive, way. All knowledge for human creatures comes through the senses. But Revelation — because it comes from God — exceeds our ability to immediately and directly grasp it. Divine Revelation is analogous to art. Imagine that you are listening to Mozart's *Jupiter Symphony*. You are asked by a friend to describe the symphony. Your own speech falters before this task. Sure, you could say something about how remarkable it is that Mozart finds a way to combine five different themes in seemingly infinite ways in the last movement of the symphony. You could describe the drama of the piece, the way that Mozart perfectly presents both darkness and light together, while never giving up hope that light conquers. None of these words is sufficient. It is only by listening to the *Jupiter Symphony*, delighting in it, and allowing oneself to perceive what is given in the performance, that we come to "hear" what there is to be heard in this great work. The work bestows itself to us, rather than the other way around. As Balthasar writes, "If Mozart's *Jupiter symphony* has a finale — which is something that I cannot anticipate, derive, or explain on the basis of anything within myself — then it can be only the finale that it has."[3] If I approach Mozart's *Jupiter* with my own master themes, rather than letting myself be taken up into the work, then it is likely that I will not hear what Mozart gives to me. So too, in God's revelation of love, if I try to capture God in categories, ideas, or images that are outside of what is revealed, then I may not perceive what God is offering.

Yet, there is a problem. There is no way for us to perceive what God offers, except through our experience. I cannot enter Mozart's mind, think what he thought, and grasp what he grasped in the act of musical composition. With God, it is even more complicated. I can read biographies of Mozart, study his composition style, become a Mozart scholar, and eventually be able to approach his work with greater understanding. I could start to think, maybe a little, like Mozart. But with God, that is impossible. It is not just that God has a different experience than I do. God is God, and I am creature. The gap between the Creator and the created is absolute — bridged only by the Incarnation of Jesus Christ.

For Balthasar, the key to "perceiving" the gift of Revelation as creature is the idea of attunement. Years ago, three-dimensional posters and images were quite popular. You stood before one of these images, looking at it, and initially saw nothing more than a random collection of shapes and colors. But as you relaxed your eyes, another image was communicated through what looked like a hodgepodge of shapes and colors. Suddenly, a shark, a bear, or a castle appeared.

Attunement, for Balthasar, is something like standing before the three-dimensional puzzle of what God has revealed. Except, one does not attune oneself. Through the gift of the Holy Spirit, we are given, by God, the capacity to perceive the form of Christ offered in the Scriptures, the sacraments, and the lives of the saints. This is what is meant by "possessing" faith. The human being is now "in-spired" (the Spirit breathes in us) through God's gift. As Balthasar writes, "The inspiration, therefore, descends upon believing man from the heights of the absolute. ... And yet, at the same time, the inspiration rises from man's own most intimate depths: it is the person himself who loves and tastes God, and not an alien principle that does this through the person."[4]

God does not reveal himself apart from our act of perceiving as a person. This means all our bodily senses, our memory, imagination, understanding, and will are involved in the act of attunement.

Thus, the sacraments objectively evangelize because they offer the person of Jesus Christ to the world through the ministry of the Church. Children become sons and daughters of the living God. The Eucharist is the sacrificial offering of Jesus Christ. The task of sacramental formation is not to make this event meaningful; it already is, because the gift is offered by the God-man, Jesus Christ. Instead, our task is one of attunement — to let men and women see in the sacraments what God is revealing. Sacraments are God's great work of art, and our full participation in them takes a lifetime of giving our bodies over to God's artistry.

We can conclude that the sacraments evangelize through

efficaciously signifying. God is active. And yet, the task of sacramental formation is to attune someone to see what is happening in the triune God's great sacramental work of art. It is here that signification is essential.

The Wondrous Meaning of the Sacred Signs

Throughout this work, we have relied on two dimensions of sacramental signs. Sacramental signs are first natural, creation sacraments that point us toward the presence of God. And sacramental signs are also historical, initiating us into salvation history.

The task of attunement requires us to more carefully attend to the sacramental signs. Here, I do not mean that sacramental formation must endlessly explain the meaning of water, light, and darkness. This kind of sacramental formation is not aesthetic, but didactic. You are left with the endless words of priests and catechists, who feel that they need to explain to you that light means hope, or that Christ is the light of the world. Through such a process of sacramental catechesis, the sacraments lose their wonder and are experienced less as God acting in the world, and more as the Church performing acts of instruction upon the faithful through matter.

Initiation into sacramental signs more fundamentally relates to cultivating meaning. Human beings today do not live in a world as if it is full of meaning. We objectify the created order. Think about how most of us treat water. Water is merely for quenching our thirst, readily available in any sink or refrigerator in our house. But how often do we spend time looking at water, attending to its details, even contemplating what water means for us?

We take what Pope Francis calls a technocratic approach to the created order, including our own lives. In his encyclical *Laudato Si'*, the Holy Father defines the technocratic paradigm as:

The way that humanity has taken up technology and its development according to an undifferentiated and one-dimensional paradigm. This paradigm exalts the concept of a subject who, using logical and rational procedures, progressively approaches and gains control over an external object. This subject makes every effort to establish the scientific and experimental method, which in itself is already a technique of possession, mastery and transformation. It is as if the subject were to find itself in the presence of something formless, completely open to manipulation. Men and women have constantly intervened in nature, but for a long time this meant being in tune with and respecting the possibilities offered by the things themselves. It was a matter of receiving what nature itself allowed, as if from its own hand. Now, by contrast, we are the ones to lay our hands on things, attempting to extract everything possible from them while frequently ignoring or forgetting the reality in front of us.[5]

In a world of technique, we do not attend first to the meaning of creation, including our fellow human beings. Rather, we use them for our own ends. There is no being present to the reality in front of us: the gift of the created order and human life. Concurrently, we do not think about ourselves as creatures in need. We are actors on the world stage, who control what is happening. We are not needy, because we are the ones who possess the power.

The sacraments of the Church make no sense in a technocratic paradigm. Water is just water, a tool that we use to make electricity. Human beings are nothing more than economic creatures, who have been made to produce and to consume. We do not think about the meaning of birth, life, and death. We participate in acts of consumerist leisure that are designed to make us forget that we possess any meaningful questions. Why be silent and wonder about the meaning of my life when I can spend hours looking at my Twitter or Instagram feed, escape into binge-watching a Netflix show, or go to a local bar and hook up with a random person?

This anti-contemplative approach to the world is deadening to human life. Although many of the instruments of technology are most often employed by young people, let us remember that it is the older generations that created this technology in the first place. We are all culpable for living in a society in which it is easier to stare at a screen than to look into the eyes of one's neighbor or to sit in wonder at the gift of creation.

The task of sacramental formation related to signs is to invite men and women to contemplate the world and their own lives as meaningful. It is to raise questions of meaning from the very beginning. For most of us, the sacraments implicitly raise questions of meaning. Parents who have a newborn babe ask themselves what it means to both nurture and educate a life. What does my life mean now that I have a child? The same goes for adolescents who are about to receive the Sacrament of Confirmation. What will my life become? At every Mass, in whatever parish, people are asking themselves the great questions of life. The Church, in her sacramental formation, must provide a space through which these questions may be asked.

Here, we possess an excellent guide in relearning a meaningful approach to sacramental formation. In a little book called *Sacred Signs*, the Catholic priest and theologian Romano Guardini invites men and women to gaze contemplatively at the sacramental signs of the Church. In discussing the Eucharistic wine, Guardini writes:

> Wine is drink. To be exact, it is more than drink, more than a liquid like water that merely quenches thirst.

"Wine that makes glad the heart of man" is the biblical expression. The purpose of wine is not only to quench thirst, but also to give pleasure and satisfaction and exhilaration. "My cup, how goodly it is, how plenteous!" Literally, how intoxicating, though not in the sense of drinking to excess. Wine possesses a sparkle, a perfume, a vigor, that expands and clears the imagination. Under the form of wine Christ gives us his divine blood. It is no plain and sober draught. It was bought at great price, at a divinely excessive price. *Sanguis Christi, inebria me,* [Blood of Christ, inebriate me] prays Saint Ignatius, that Knight of the Burning Heart.[6]

Notice Guardini's approach. He attends closely to wine as a sign, infused with meaning. The Scriptures themselves recognize the festivity of wine. Wine sparkles, has a sweet perfume, and is employed by men and women in festive situations. When we recognize all these dimensions of wine, we see anew what it means to say that Christ gives his Body and Blood through the species of bread and wine. To drink Christ's Blood in the Sacrament of the Eucharist is to delight in the gift of wine.

If we are to dispose the faithful to recognize the gift of the created order that is taken up in the sacramental economy of the Church, then we must think anew about the frenetic pace of most sacramental preparation. Information is shared in dingy church basements without time to contemplate what *everything* means. Here, sacramental preparation must cultivate festivity in its fullest sense. Festivity is not a consumeristic approach to leisure. Instead, it is the willingness to take the time to behold, to gaze as an act of love. As the Catholic philosopher Josef Pieper comments:

From this it follows that the concept of festivity is inconceivable without an element of contemplation. ... It means a relaxing of the strenuous fixation of the eye on the given frame of reference, without which no utilitarian act is accomplished. Instead, the field of vision widens, concern for success or failure of an act falls away, and the soul turns to its infinite object; it becomes aware of the illimitable horizon of reality as a whole.[7]

Sacramental preparation should be a loving contemplation of the natural signs, which are taken up into salvation history. Adults have a good deal to learn from Sofia Cavalletti's Catechesis of the Good Shepherd — a Montessorian approach to catechesis that cultivates dispositions of wonder, festivity, joy, and contemplation as the young child savors the mystery of salvation in the Scriptures and the liturgy.[8]

The Sacraments and the Personal Drama of Salvation

The sacred signs of the sacraments, though, cannot be understood exclusively in an aesthetic mode. It is not just that we look at the sacraments. We have a role to play through participation in the sacramental life. In other words, the sacraments are not only like a painting where the divine artist reveals to us the meaning of existence, but they are also a drama in which I take up my role as an adopted son or daughter of the Father.

The main character in the drama of the sacramental life is not us. Rather, it is God. In the very first chapter, we saw that the sacramental signs initiate us into salvation history. When I am baptized, I participate in Christ's own baptism in the river Jordan. I become a son of God through my union with Jesus Christ. Confirmation is a maturation of this union, a new gift of the Spirit that sends me out to consecrate every aspect of creation to the Father. In the Eucharistic Sacrifice of Christ, I not only participate in the self-giving love of Jesus Christ upon the cross, but I am nourished by his Eucharistic Body. My life is taken up into his — he consumes me. The Sacrament of Holy Orders takes up the personality of a mere man who now is bestowed a gift of divine love by God so that he may speak in the words of Christ, as well as teach and govern as Jesus Christ in the Church. Through matrimony, the couple's own drama of love is knit into the love of Christ and the Church, the grace of that love infusing the most natural of human relationships. Family life is a participation in a divine drama, the triune God manifesting himself in every corner of the world. Penance transforms the drama of my own conversion, enabling me to participate anew in the Eucharistic drama of the Church. The anointing of the sick is Jesus Christ's consecration of the drama of sickness and death, one that every human being will undergo.

To dispose men and women to participate fully in the sacraments, we must contemplate within the Church the drama of salvation history. Sacramentality is not reducible to God's general presence in creation. Sacramentality involves the mystery hidden from the foundation of the world (cf. Col 1:26), Jesus Christ, who is the image of the invisible God. The sacraments make available the life of Christ in the world, and the more we contemplate every dimension of his life, the more we recognize the gift of love that is offered in the first place. The Word of God is integral to the sacraments. The Scriptures are not just a guidebook for life. They manifest to us the wondrous deeds that God has accomplished, while also inviting us to see how God still wants to work *here and now*. Sacramental formation is Scriptural formation.

And yet, we have a role to play in the drama of the sacramental. The Scriptures and the sacraments alike are an invitation from God, not a totalitarian program of forced grace. The theologian Francesca Murphy comments on this freedom of the human being vis-à-vis salvation history:

To will the good of another is to want them to be themselves, to permit them freely to move towards their own
good. Human beings do not merely have an inbuilt "ori-
entation" towards the divine revelation; they have to
be asked; only an "invitation" respects their freedom. If
God's self-disclosure respects the freedom of its human
recipient, so it also springs out of his own freedom.[9]

In much of modern life, we feel that we have little freedom. The
adolescent assumes that her happiness is dependent on the pursuit of a career that generates a fortune. The young man is initiated into a story in which he is told that he must hook up with
as many women as possible. The minimum wage worker sees
a life of hard labor ahead of him, no escape from a work-a-day
world in which he can barely afford his monthly rent and a bit
of food. This lack of freedom is debilitating and fundamentally
dehumanizing.

The sacramental system is a gift because it bestows back to
us not a mere human freedom, but the very freedom of the God-
man, Jesus Christ. The gift of character in the sacraments changes our identity, while also bestowing upon us the freedom to turn
our lives into a sacrifice of love. Original sin is washed away in
baptism so that we may offer our lives in total freedom to the
God who is love. The sacramentally initiated Christian — who
is baptized, confirmed, and who regularly receives the Eucharist
— has both the freedom and the mission to sanctify the whole
world to God. There is no aspect of his or her drama that is entirely bereft or absent of God's own dramatic redemption. The
sacramentalized Christian exists in God's own free gift of love.

We must, then, in sacramental formation, bestow upon men
and women the freedom of the self-giving love of the sacraments.
And yet, the pedagogy by which we often approach sacramental
formation is surprisingly *nonfreeing*. Parishes often create reg-

ulations for the reception of the sacraments that force parents and young children to "earn" sacramental grace. Not a few parishes and dioceses have argued that confirmation *must* occur in adolescence so that children *must* stay in the Church through at least their seventeenth year. In such instances, confirmation becomes a stick without a carrot.

There are indeed laws governing the reception of the sacraments. The Church should follow these laws. But there is a danger of creating additional, even excessive, laws for the reception of a sacrament. A parish that says a couple must be registered for nine months before the baptism of a child has created a regulation that is both unnecessary and a denial of the gift of love to a child.

The task of the catechist must be to communicate the freedom that is possible in receiving a sacrament. Take confirmation. Whether one is confirming at the age of seven or eighteen, the sacrament should be presented as a gift of divine love that sends the young child or adolescent out on mission. The young child, who is discovering for the first time true freedom, receives in this sacrament the capacity to grow into perfect love through a wise use of that freedom. The young child may be challenged to sanctify the world through his or her freedom in the family sphere. An adolescent can also receive this sacrament as a great gift of freedom, consecrating school and friendships to Christ. Likely, the adolescent has abused freedom in ways that the seven-year-old has not. But also, the adolescent, awakening to even deeper questions through natural development, has the growing capacity to freely participate in the apostolic nature of the Church. The adolescent may choose to get up early in the morning and go to Mass to sanctify the day to God.

What God ultimately gives in the sacraments, in each one of them, is a renewal of our freedom as creatures made in the image and likeness of God. The renewal of culture, even our public life, necessitates the priestly use of this freedom. The sacraments enable men and women to offer their entire lives as a gift of love. The name for this offering is worship. The drama of every human life involves what, and how, we will worship with the fullness of our beings. If sacramental formation treats the sacraments as nothing more than nice little rituals in an otherwise secular life, then we should not be surprised that people have stopped coming to the sacraments. Sacramental formation must dispose us to see our lives, in their entirety, as a free act of worship to God — as a participation in the drama of the priesthood of all believers.

And it is for this reason that the sacramental life extends beyond participation in the sacraments alone. Marriage, as you remember, incarnates this principle. The consent of marriage is not reserved to a moment in time, but is to transform every aspect of the couple into a sacrifice of love. The couple "becomes" a sacrament in the world. And as a sacrament, the couple bears fruit insofar as they live their marriage and family life in light of their deepest identity. Through the gift of the nuptial bond, the couple does not live out this identity exclusively within the home. Everywhere the domestic church goes, they have a mission to share divine love with the world.

What is true of the Sacrament of Marriage is true of all those Christians who are baptized, confirmed, and who regularly receive the Eucharist. Christian identity is not only for Sunday mornings. Rather, through immersion into the drama of Christ himself, the Catholic is to become an efficacious sign in the world. There is a public dimension to sacramental participation. The Christian who receives the Blessed Sacrament on a Sunday morning is called to create a world governed not by scarcity, but total, self-giving love. The grace of the Eucharist, the gift of divine life, sends the whole Body of Christ on this Eucharistic mission. The Catholic who is baptized, confirmed, and strengthened by the Eucharist feeds the hungry, stands up for the rights of the unborn, is concerned about the welfare of the prisoner, speaks out against racism, and offers hospitality to the migrant, because he or she has received the fullness of love in the sacramental life. These public acts of witness, even perhaps unto death itself in the case of martyrdom, are the return-gift of love that the sacramentalized, absolutely free, and indeed very evangelized Catholic offers to the world.

Conclusion

Throughout, this book has focused on the sacraments as a participation in the life of the God-man, Jesus Christ. This participation takes up human life, consecrates it to God, and then sends the Christian out on mission to make his or her life a living sacrifice of love. The sacramental life of the Church is intrinsically evangelizing, restoring creation to its original destiny. And this destiny is to create a world ordered not to violence, force, scarcity, or any of the other wages of sin and death. Instead, the sacramental world is a space for worship, freedom, and love. There is perhaps nothing more evangelizing, in the end, than the sacraments — at least until we see God face-to-face in the communion of saints. Until then, what a gift we have received from God in the sacraments.

Acknowledgments

To my undergraduate students at the University of Notre Dame who have asked me again and again why the sacraments matter. Your patience with my stumbling responses, and our common dialogue, enabled me to write this book. Through the publication of this book, I am looking forward to continuing the dialogue.

Notes

Introduction

1. Center for Applied Research in the Apostolate, "Frequently Requested Church Statistics," https://cara.georgetown.edu/frequently -requested-church-statistics/.

2. *Directory for Catechesis* (Washington D.C.: United States Conference of Catholic Bishops, 2020), no. 30.

Chapter 1: Sacramentalized and Evangelized

1. *Catechism of the Catholic Church*, no. 1131.

2. Joseph Ratzinger, "Typos, Mysterium, Sacramentum: The Sacramental Foundation of Christian Existence," in *Theology of the Liturgy: The Sacramental Foundation of Christian Existence*, trans. John Seward, Kenneth Baker, SJ, Henry Taylor, et al. (San Francisco: Ignatius Press, 2014), 158.

3. Ratzinger, "Typos, Mysterium, Sacramentum," 162.

4. CCC 481.

5. Matthias Scheeben, *The Mysteries of Christianity*, trans. Cyril Vollert, SJ (New York: Crossroad, 2006), 331.

6. Literally, the Paschal Mystery means Christ's "Passover" (his Pascha) from death into new life.

7. Scheeben, *The Mysteries of Christianity*, 437.

8. *Lumen Gentium*, no. 7.

9. Thomas Aquinas, *Summa Theologiae*, III. q.65, c.

10. Scheeben, *The Mysteries of Christianity*, 571.

11. Ibid., 17.

Chapter 2: Our Identity as Priests of Christ: Baptism, Confirmation, and Holy Orders

1. *Lumen Gentium*, no. 10.

2. CCC 121.

3. Jean Daniélou, SJ, *The Bible and the Liturgy* (Notre Dame, IN: University of Notre Dame, 2009), 68.

4. Matthias Scheeben, *The Mysteries of Christianity*, trans. Cyril Vollert, SJ (New York: Crossroad Publishing Company, 2006), 582–583.

5. Ibid., 583.

6. Maxwell Johnson, *The Rites of Christian Initiation: Their Evolution and Interpretation*, 2nd ed. (Collegeville, MN: Liturgical Press), 159–200.

7. A new, English translation of the RCIA is in progress, to be called *The Order of Christian Initiation of Adults*.

8. For a commentary on these rites, see Timothy P. O'Malley, *Divine Blessing: Liturgical Formation in the R.C.I.A.* (Collegeville, MN: Liturgical Press, 2019).

9. CCC 1214–1216.

10. Robin Jensen, *Baptismal Imagery in Early Christianity: Ritual, Visual, and Theological Dimensions* (Grand Rapids, MI: Baker Academic, 2012).

11. CCC 1216.

12. Joseph Ratzinger, *The God of Jesus Christ: Meditations on the Triune God* (San Francisco: Ignatius Press, 2018), 35.

13. Kimberly H. Belcher, *Efficacious Engagement: Sacramental Participation in the Trinitarian Mystery* (Collegeville, MN: Liturgical Press, 2012), 128–155.

14. CCC 1265.

15. For a history of Confirmation in the twentieth century, see Timothy R. Gabrielli, *Confirmation: How a Sacrament of God's Grace Became All About Us* (Collegeville, MN: Liturgical Press, 2013).

16. CCC 1293.

17. Ibid., no. 1294.

18. For a defense of the development of orders, see Matthew Levering, *Christ and the Catholic Priesthood: Ecclesial Hierarchy and the*

Pattern of the Trinity (Chicago: Hillebrand Books, 2010), 120–182.

19. Jean-Pierre Torrell, *A Priestly People: Baptismal Priesthood and Priestly Ministry*, trans. Peter Heinegg (New York: Paulist Press, 2013), 84.

20. CCC 1547.

21. Ibid., no. 1554.

22. Nicole Winfield, "Pope creates new expert commission to study women deacons," *Crux*. https://cruxnow.com/vatican/2020/04/pope-creates-new-expert-commission-to-study-women-deacons/.

23. Sara Butler, MSBT, *The Catholic Priesthood and Women: A Guide to the Teaching of the Church* (Chicago: Hillebrand Books, 2006), 13–14.

24. Ibid., 90.

25. Jean-Pierre Torrell, *A Priestly People*, 189.

Chapter 3: The Eucharist and the Sacrifice of Time

1. Jan-Heiner Tück, *A Gift of Presence: The Theology and Poetry of the Eucharist in Thomas Aquinas*, trans. Scott G. Hefelfinger (Washington, DC: Catholic University of America Press, 2018).

2. Aquinas, *ST*, III. q.73. 4, corpus.

3. Timothy P. O'Malley, *Liturgy and the New Evangelization: Practicing the Art of Self-Giving Love*, 76–107.

4. CCC 1104.

5. See Joseph Ratzinger, *Jesus of Nazareth, Part Two: Holy Week from the Entrance into Jerusalem to the Resurrection* (San Francisco: Ignatius Press, 2010), 106–114.

6. Joseph Ratzinger, *The Eucharist: Heart of the Church*, in *Joseph Ratzinger: Collected Works—Theology of the Liturgy* (San Francisco: Ignatius Press, 2014), 261.

7. Ibid., 267.

8. For an excellent introduction to the doctrines of real presence and transubstantiation, I recommend James Thomas O'Connor, *The Hidden Manna: A Theology of the Eucharist* (San Francisco: Ignatius

Press, 2005). Also, see Timothy P. O'Malley, *Real Presence: What Does It Mean and Why Does It Matter?* (Notre Dame, IN: Ave Maria Press, 2021).

9. Incidentally, we do not own a dog. This is a sore point for my daughter.

10. CCC 1376.

11. Scheeben, *The Mysteries of Christianity,* 484.

12. CCC 1391–1401.

13. Dorothy Day, *The Long Loneliness* (San Francisco: Harper-One, 1996), 285–286.

14. Joseph Ratzinger, *The Spirit of the Liturgy,* in *Joseph Ratzinger: Collected Works—Theology of the Liturgy,* 30.

15. Benedict XVI, *Sacramentum Caritatis,* no. 71. http://www.vatican.va/content/benedict-xvi/en/apost_exhortations/documents/hf_ben-xvi_exh_20070222_sacramentum-caritatis.html#The_eucharistic_form_of_the_christian_life.

Chapter 4: Marriage as the Transformation of the Mundane

1. Augustine, *The Excellence of Marriage,* in *Marriage and Virginity,* trans. Ray Kearney (Hyde Park, NY: New City Press, 1999), 1.1–18.22.

2. Many of these early marriage liturgies may be found in *Documents of the Marriage Liturgy,* ed. Mark Searle and Kenneth W. Stevenson (Collegeville, MN: Liturgical Press, 1992).

3. Phillip Reynolds, *How Marriage Became One of the Sacraments: The Sacramental Theology of Marriage from Its Medieval Origins to the Council of Trent* (New York: Cambridge University Press, 2016), 209–243.

4. Jean LeClercq, *Monks on Marriage, A Twelfth Century View* (New York: Seabury Press, 1982).

5. Bernard of Clairvaux, Sermon 2.2 in *Song of Songs* I, trans. Kilian Walsh, OCSCO (Kalamazoo, MI: Cistercian Publications, 1971), 9.

6. Ann W. Astell, *The Song of Songs in the Middle Ages* (Ithaca, NY: Cornell University Press, 1995).

7. Hugh of St. Victor, *On the Sacraments*, II, 11, III.

8. Bonaventure, *Breviloquium, VI, 13, 2.*

9. Thomas Aquinas, *Summa Contra Gentiles, IV, 78, 4.*

10. Scheeben, *The Mysteries of Christianity*, trans. Cyril Vollert, SJ (New York: Crossroad, 2006), 605–606.

11. "Be subject to one another out of reverence for Christ. Wives, be subject to your husbands, as to the Lord. For the husband is the head of the wife as Christ is the head of the church, his body, and is himself its Savior. As the church is subject to Christ, so let wives also be subject in everything to their husbands. Husbands, love your wives, as Christ loved the church and gave himself up for her, that he might sanctify her, having cleansed her by the washing of water with the word, that he might present the church to himself in splendor, without spot or wrinkle or any such thing, that she might be holy and without blemish. Even so husbands should love their wives as their own bodies. He who loves his wife loves himself. For no man ever hates his own flesh, but nourishes and cherishes it, as Christ does the church, because we are members of his body. 'For this reason a man shall leave his father and mother and be joined to his wife, and the two shall become one flesh.' This mystery is a profound one, and I am saying that it refers to Christ and the church; however, let each one of you love his wife as himself, and let the wife see that she respects her husband" (Eph. 5:21-33; RSV).

12. John Paul II, *The Theology of the Body* (Boston: Pauline Books & Media), 352.

13. Cardinal Marc Ouellet, *Mystery and Sacrament of Love: A Theology of Marriage and the Family for the New Evangelization*, trans. Michelle K. Borras and Adrian J. Walker (Grand Rapids, MI: Eerdmans, 2014), 63.

14. Ibid., 70.

15. John Grabowski, *Sex and Virtue: An Introduction to Sexual*

Ethics (Washington DC: Catholic University of America Press, 2003), 43–48.

16. Ouellet, *Mystery and Sacrament of Love*, 80.

17. Ibid., 80.

18. Ibid., 95.

19. Timothy P. O'Malley, *Off the Hook: God, Love, Dating, and Marriage in a Hookup World* (Notre Dame, IN: Ave Maria Press, 2018).

20. Timothy P. O'Malley, "Learning to Dwell with the Beloved: The Wisdom of the Marriage Liturgy," in *Sex, Love, and Families: Catholic Perspectives*, ed. Jason King and Julie Hanlon Rubio (Collegeville, MN: Liturgical Press, 2020), 139–149.

21. Ouellet, *Mystery and Sacrament of Love*, 99.

22. Ibid., 104.

23. Timothy P. O'Malley, "The Liturgical-Sacramental Identity of the Domestic Church: Combatting Domestic Romanticism by Means of the Liturgical Act," *Antiphon* 24, 1 (2020) 1—18.

24. Angelo Scola, *Nuptial Mystery*, trans. Michelle K. Borras (Grand Rapids, MI: Eerdmans, 2005), 307.

Chapter 5 : Sin and Death: Consecrating Our Diminishments

1. Teilhard de Chardin, SJ, *The Divine Milieu: An Essay on the Interior Life* (New York: Harper Torchbooks, 1965), 81–82.

2. Joseph Ratzinger, *'In the Beginning...': A Catholic Understanding of the Story of Creation and the Fall*, trans. Boniface Ramsey, OP (Grand Rapids, MI: Eerdmans, 1995), 70.

3. Gary A. Anderson, *The Genesis of Perfection* (Louisville, KY: Westminster John Knox, 2001), 121.

4. Paul S. Minear, *To Heal and to Reveal: The Prophetic Vocation According to Luke* (New York: The Seabury Press, 1976), 73.

5. Bruce T. Morrill, SJ, "Christ the Healer: An Investigation of Contemporary Liturgical, Pastoral, and Biblical Approaches," in *Prac-*

ticing Catholic: Ritual, Body, and Contestation in Catholic Faith, ed. Bruce Morrill, Joanna E. Ziegler, and Susan Rodgers (New York: Palgrave Macmillan, 2006), 127–128.

6. Joseph Ratzinger, *Eschatology: Death and Eternal Life*, 2nd ed., trans. Michael Waldstein (Washington DC: Catholic University of America Press, 1988), 93.

7. Hans Urs von Balthasar, *Life Out of Death: Meditations on the Paschal Mystery*, trans. Martina Stöckl (San Francisco: Ignatius Press, 2012), 38–39.

8. Antonio Santantoni, "Reconciliation in the First Four Centuries," in *Sacraments and Sacramentals, Handbook for Liturgical Studies—Volume IV* (Collegeville, MN: Liturgical Press, 2000), 93.

9. Antonio Santantoni, "Reconciliation in the West," in *Sacraments and Sacramentals*, 135–136.

10. Ibid., 146.

11. CCC 1423.

12. Scheeben, *The Mysteries of Christianity*, 246–247.

13. CCC 1437.

14. For those interested in seeing how this "liturgical form" of life might be lived out, see David W. Fagerberg, *On Liturgical Asceticism* (Washington, DC: Catholic University of America Press, 2013).

15. CCC 1459.

16. Teresa of Ávila, *The Way of Perfection*, trans. Kieran Kavanaugh (Washington, DC: Institute for Carmelite Studies, 2000), 289.

17. Scheeben, *The Mysteries of Christianity*, 577.

18. *The Pastoral Care of the Sick*, in *The Rites of the Catholic Church—Volume 1* (Collegeville, MN: Liturgical Press, 1990), no. 1.

19. Phillipe Rouillard, OSB, "The Anointing of the Sick in the West," in *Sacraments and Sacramentals*, 171–190.

20. Thomas Aquinas, *Summa Contra Gentiles*, IV, 74, 3.

21. Scheeben, *Mysteries of Christianity*, 577.

22. *Pastoral Care of the Sick*, no. 125C.

23. Bruce T. Morrill, *Divine Worship and Human Healing: Litur-*

gical Theology at the Margins of Life and Death (Collegeville, MN: Liturgical Press, 2009), 162–165.

24. James T. O'Connor, *The Hidden Manna: A Theology of the Eucharist* (San Francisco: St. Ignatius Press, 2005), 305–306.

Chapter 6: Cultivating Dispositions for a Sacramental Life

1. *Directory for Catechesis* (Washington, DC: United States Conference of Catholic Bishops, 2020), no. 29.

2. Aaron B. Seligman, Robert P. Weller, Michael J. Puett, and Bennett Simon, *Ritual and Its Consequences: An Essay on the Limits of Sincerity* (New York: Oxford University Press, 2008), 116.

3. Hans Urs von Balthasar, *Love Alone Is Credible*, trans. D. C. Schindler (San Francisco: Ignatius Press, 1963), 53.

4. Hans Urs von Balthasar, *The Glory of the Lord, Volume 1: Seeing the Form*, trans. Erasmo Leiva-Merikakis (San Francisco: Ignatius Press, 1982), 250.

5. Pope Francis, *Laudato Si'*, no. 106.

6. Romano Guardini, *Sacred Signs*, trans. Grace Branham (St. Louis, MO: Pio Decimo Press, 1956), 38.

7. Josef Pieper, *In Tune with the World: A Theory of Festivity* (South Bend, IN: St. Augustine's Press, 1999), 16.

8. The theological and philosophical foundation to this approach may be found in Sofia Cavalletti, *The Religious Potential of the Child—Volume 1*, trans. Patricia M. Coulter and Julie M. Coulter (Chicago: Liturgical Training Publications, 1992); for an excellent introduction to this approach in catechesis, see Jessica Keating, "Catechesis of the Good Shepherd: Cultivating the Christian Imagination of the Child," *Church Life Journal*, January 23, 2017. https://churchlifejournal.nd.edu/articles/catechesis-of-the-good-shepherd-cultivating-the-christian-imagination-of-the-child/.

9. Francesca Murphy, *The Comedy of Revelation: Paradise Lost and Regained in Biblical Narrative* (Edinburgh: T&T Clark, 2000), 341.

About the Author

Timothy P. O'Malley, Ph.D., is director of digital learning at the McGrath Institute for Church Life, where he also serves as the academic director of the Notre Dame Center for Liturgy. He teaches and researches in liturgical-sacramental theology, marriage and family, catechesis, and Catholic education. In addition to his work at Notre Dame, Prof. O'Malley serves as a member of the executive team of the USCCB's Eucharistic Revival and as a member of the mission committee of the University of the Incarnate Word's board of trustees in San Antonio, TX. He is married to Kara and has two children.